Collaborating with Strangers

W9-BBW-189

Collaborating with Strangers

Facilitating Workshops in Libraries, Classes, and Nonprofits

A How-To-Do-It Manual for Librarians®

Bess G. de Farber, April Hines, and Barbara J. Hood

Neal-Schuman

An imprint of the American Library Association

CHICAGO 2017

© 2017 by the American Library Association

Extensive effort has gone into ensuring the reliability of the information in this book; however, the publisher makes no warranty, express or implied, with respect to the material contained herein.

CoLAB Planning Series®, a registered trademark, was developed by professional facilitator and nonprofit management expert Bess G. de Farber.

ISBN: 978-0-8389-1542-4 (paper)

Library of Congress Cataloging-in-Publication Data

Names: de Farber, Bess G., 1956- author. | Hines, April, author. | Hood, Barbara J., author.
Title: Collaborating with strangers : facilitating workshops in libraries, classes, and nonprofits / Bess G. de Farber, April Hines, Barbara J. Hood.
Description: Chicago : ALA Neal-Schuman, an imprint of the American Library Association, [2017] | Series: A how-to-do-it manual for librarians | Includes bibliographical references and index.
Identifiers: LCCN 2016058526 | ISBN 9780838915424 (pbk. : alk. paper)
Subjects: LCSH: Libraries and community. | Workshops (Adult education)—Planning. | Library institutes and workshops—Planning. | Conversation. | Cooperation. | Creative thinking.
Classification: LCC Z716.4 .D423 2017 | DDC 021.2—dc23 LC record available at https://lccn.loc.gov/2016058526

Cover design by Alejandra Diaz. Text composed in Minion Pro and Interstate typefaces.

♾ This paper meets the requirements of ANSI/NISO Z39.48–1992 (Permanence of Paper).

Printed in the United States of America
21 20 19 18 17   5 4 3 2 1

*To all who have supported and participated in CoLAB Planning Series Workshops and,
most especially, to Casandra Tanenbaum and Glen Boecher
for unwaveringly contributing their extraordinary assets*

*And to Joseph Farber (1901–1972), a Polish immigrant who came through Ellis Island
and never met a stranger he couldn't talk to*

Contents

Preface

The power of combining forces with diverse partners for planning and actualizing innovative projects can hardly be overstated. Not only does working together reduce duplication of effort, but the synergy of collaboration stimulates creativity and maximizes the collective impact of combined assets. Recognizing the emphasis on developing collaborative programs and projects in nonprofit and academic settings, *Collaborating with Strangers: Facilitating Workshops in Libraries, Classes, and Nonprofits* seeks to inspire and guide those in libraries—as well as in museums, classrooms, and all types of nonprofit organizations—to promote, facilitate, and evaluate collaboration development workshops in their own communities.

Finding appropriate partners with access to the resources required to advance any project or program can be difficult. Whether those potential partners are well-known, have loose ties, or are complete strangers to us, identifying them—and discovering that you share fundamental interests and have enthusiasm for combining complementary skills and assets to achieve your common goals—is often an elusive dream.

This book shares step-by-step best practices for facilitating workshops to initiate, in real time, collaborative relationships that otherwise likely would never materialize. Workshops in the CoLAB Planning Series® (CoLAB Workshops) create comfortable environments for meeting strangers. They already have served hundreds of organizations and thousands of participants—including nonprofit staff and volunteers, students, faculty, academic administrators, and many staff members at libraries. Librarians and library staff members, as trusted and neutral information stewards, have proven to be ideal conveners for these workshops. Other highly effective conveners have included leaders of community foundations, United Ways, and nonprofit resource centers.

Except perhaps for those studying or working in fields like marketing and communication, most of us tend to avoid talking or working directly with others we do not know. Current literature confirms this growing trend. Consistent with what previously has been written on this topic, we have amassed an abundance of first-hand information on the subject from participants who have completed CoLAB Workshops. Through survey responses and other feedback, CoLAB participants overwhelmingly indicate a pervasive reluctance to speak with strangers, while also expressing enthusiasm and gratitude for the CoLAB experience in helping to overcome these barriers. Participant feedback invariably reaffirms the multiple benefits produced by these workshop strategies, which give people permission to be themselves while at the same time supporting conversations that quickly share hidden assets—the fuel for moving projects and people forward.

In this book, we share everything about the processes for presenting, promoting, acquiring sponsorship for, and evaluating these workshops so that others will be motivated and prepared to deliver their own CoLABs with confidence, either within their own communities or at conferences, and in classrooms anywhere. Beyond introducing readers to the activities facilitated during CoLAB Planning Series Workshops, *Collaborating with Strangers* shares evidence of beneficial outcomes, detailed guidance for presenting workshops, and a compilation of lessons learned from past workshops.

Throughout, chapters include how-to instructions for the two flavors of CoLAB Workshops: (1) those convening individuals who will be sharing their own personal and professional interests and (2) those for organizations where participants will be representing the interests, programs, and operations of an organization. Many types of situations in which each of these two workshop varieties can be usefully applied are explored in detail.

Organization

Collaborating with Strangers: Facilitating Workshops in Libraries, Classes, and Nonprofits includes eight chapters that progress from discussing concepts about why engaging strangers in face-to-face conversations is essential in forming new partnerships to presenting the complete and detailed steps required to execute various scenarios of workshops designed for different types of participants or circumstances—all derived from actual workshop experiences. Photographs, flowcharts, floor plans, and other figures are included to provide additional visual context.

Rather than reading from cover to cover, we suggest that you read the details provided in chapter 4 when your team is ready to use this information as a step-by-step guide for planning your own CoLAB Workshop.

Chapter 1, "The Importance of Strangers and Face-to-Face Conversations," shares a few vignettes presented to highlight the many benefits of combining forces with others—whether known or unknown, within or outside disciplines—toward advancing goals and improving quality of life.

Chapter 2, "Introduction to CoLAB Workshops," leads you through visualizations of two past CoLAB Workshops, one that was presented for organization representatives who were interested in jump-starting partnerships in communities near Lake Okeechobee, Florida; and another that was designed for faculty, students, and administrators who were interested in combining forces around the topic of sustainability at the University of Florida. This chapter documents the history of how these workshops were initiated and the guiding principles and conditions that enabled their successful delivery. Information about strategies for creating effective "profile-signs" describes the centerpiece of these workshops. We also present a case for why libraries and library employees are best suited to convene and facilitate these workshops.

Chapter 3, "CoLAB Workshop Assessments, Results, and Participant Stories," describes, in the voices of attendees, the many results that workshops have produced, both for organization representatives and for individual participants. Descriptions of methods that have been used for acquiring this feedback provide ideas for how your team can gather data relating to workshop effectiveness, even for discovering the stories that evolve months or years after the workshops take place.

Chapter 4, "Step-by-Step Instructions for Conducting CoLAB Workshops," guides you through four distinct workshops presented in (1) an on-campus environment, (2) an academic library, (3) a classroom as part of a course, and (4) a community location. Each workshop features a different purpose. The steps—for preworkshop, during the workshop, and postworkshop activities, illustrated through detailed agendas, flow-charts, floor plans, and photographs—show how each workshop can be customized. The individual scenarios seek to maximize benefits for a variety of participant types, including faculty, academic administrators, students, librarians, library staff members, and nonprofit organization representatives.

Chapter 5, "Variations on CoLAB Workshop Activities," outlines the different options for presenting CoLAB activities within meetings or conferences and also describes strategies for CoLAB Workshops that highlight a specific topic, are designed for a specific geographic region, are intended to facilitate matchmaking across disciplines or for mentorship, or aim to encourage new partnerships for inclusion in grant proposals.

Chapter 6, "Seeking Sponsors for CoLAB Workshops," breaks down the process for acquiring external support or resources. Included are excerpts from awarded grant proposals that have funded workshop activities and strategies for requesting in-kind contributions from corporate donors.

Chapter 7, "Promotional Strategies for CoLAB Workshops," offers detailed instructions for designing and pushing out promotional materials, for designing a dedicated CoLAB Workshop website, and for using social media for postworkshop connections. Examples of past workshop materials illustrate how design elements effectively come together and provide you with visual models.

Chapter 8, "Tips and Lessons Learned for Presenting Successful CoLAB Workshops," makes recommendations on how to handle twenty different situations that may arise before, during, or after the workshop. These recommendations were generated from actual workshop experiences.

CoLAB Workshop facilitative processes create opportunities for librarians, library staff members, and those outside the library world to embrace their evolving new roles as conveners and facilitators. Considering the ever-growing tendency to communicate electronically, CoLAB Workshops offer a proven method of reintegrating real-time, face-to-face conversations into classrooms, conferences, and communities and generating innovation while revealing the wealth of resources available for those who choose to become involved.

Acknowledgments

We are tremendously grateful to all who have assisted in developing, coordinating, promoting, evaluating, and co-facilitating the CoLAB Planning Series Workshops: Sophia Acord, Jessica Albano, Ricardo Andrade, Rebecca Barham, Dina Benson, Rebecca Blakiston, Timothy Blanton, Denise Bookwalter, Leticia Boswell, Karen Brooks, Dana Bublitz, Amy Buhler, Douglas Campbell, Jessica Childers, Robin Chin-Roemer, Missy Clapp, Gloria Colvin, Cindy Craig, Jaret Daniels, Elise Doney, Mary Edwards, Bonnie Effros, Bridget Elmer, Jennifer Gillett-Kaufman, Ann Gleason, Sara Russell Gonzalez, Louise Grant, Stephanie Haas, Caroline Hallman, Carol Hargis, Chloe Horning, Robin Huff-Eibl, Nancy Huling, Barbara Hutchinson, Rae Jesano, Lela Johnson, Margeaux Johnson, Brian Keith, Emily Keller, Spencer Keralis, Spiro Kiousis, Elizabeth Kline, Ellen Knudson, Kevin Knudson, Janice Kreiger, Ann Lally, Lucinda Lavelli, Sarah Leadley, Michael LeDuc, Sofia Leung, Ann Lindell, Nargiza Ludgate, Dorothy MacDiarmid, Catherine Macy, Donald McGlothlin, Laura McKinnon, David Miller, Juan-Carlos Molleda, Jo Monahan, Jenny Muilenberg, Barbara Noble, Hannah Norton, Gregory Orloff, Erin O'Toole, Matt Parsons, Jeanne Pfander, Shelley Phipps, Lauren Ray, Patrick Reakes, Diane Robson, Lylly Rodriguez, Melody Royster, Judith Russell, Nancy Schaefer, Elivio Serrano, Susan Smith, Kimberly Sovenski, George Sparks, Carol Spring, MJ Steele, Nina Stoyan-Rosenzweig, Casandra Tanenbaum, Laurie Taylor, Michele Tennant, Anne Marie Thigpen, Beth Thomsett, Debbie Treise, Amy Vigilante, Barbara Volkmann, Angela Weaver, Donna Wrublewski, Mary Wyns, and Hannah Vander Zanden.

Special thanks to student assistants at the University of Florida: Daniel Azneer, Logan Jaffe, Alexandrea Matthews, Venkitachalam Parameswaran, Kirtana Rajan, Tirumala Tumati, and Suchitra Yellapantula.

The Importance of Strangers and Face-to-Face Conversations

Although we are all strangers, it seems that "strangers" in society have been getting a bad rap for quite some time. The "Don't talk to strangers" mantra that has permeated our culture can actually be a very unfortunate instruction. Strangers have always played, and always will play, vital roles in our lives.

Every one of us inevitably comes into physical proximity with others we do not know. Each of these strangers carries with him or her a rich, varied history and a unique set of personal assets. So how can we come to know about those with whom we have never engaged? Can you recall the last time you noticed a stranger, listened to him or her, watched that person work? We may tend to make quick judgments about others based on nothing more than a momentary glimpse. You could probably invent a story about each stranger from just one instance. Would it be correct or complete? Rationally, we know this type of quick assessment can lead to all sorts of wrong assumptions, distortions, and inaccurate conclusions about these people. We do it so fast—automatically for many of us.

Deliberately Connecting with Strangers

Not many people knew Oseola McCarty, who grew up and lived near the University of Southern Mississippi in Hattiesburg. She was born in 1908 and finished the fifth grade. She was a washerwoman, doing laundry for others to support herself, and also to save. Without meeting McCarty, who never married and had no children, it would have been impossible to know the truth about what was important to her. In 1995, McCarty retired and donated $150,000 to the University of Southern Mississippi to be used for scholarships for students who otherwise would not be able to enroll. Word of McCarty's contribution inspired 600 others in Hattiesburg to join her effort, tripling the value of her gift.[1]

In effect, McCarty's lifelong project was to help others succeed in acquiring an education. When others met her, through the news media, she was transformed from an unknown, a stranger, into someone worthy of engaging collaborators, simply by sharing information about her assets and her wish to share them in a way that supported what she was most passionate about: giving others the opportunity to acquire an education.

The challenges that we experience in talking to or working with people we do not know can emerge in countless situations. Consider the curriculum vitae or résumé—a document detailing employment history as well as the many assets that might be shared by a potential new employee. After making the hire, what happens to this document? In most work environments, it disappears; in others, it can be freely accessed but doesn't get used. Unfortunately, these documents are not valued for the wealth of information they invariably contain. Without knowing a new hire's history and assets, colleagues have to start from scratch to learn all that a new employee is capable of contributing, accessing, communicating, and so forth. How long would it take, how many meetings or one-on-one lunches, to learn about these past and current assets so that the new hire can be assimilated into the workplace? It could take forever and likely would never be accomplished. It has probably happened to you many times, whether as a new employee or as a co-worker whose job it is to work successfully with a new hire.

Let's exam a theoretical framework advanced by Gareth Morgan, author of *Images of Organization*, supporting the premise that connecting with strangers, or folks with whom we have loose ties, in fact produces more innovative ideas while enhancing what happens in the workplace.[2] Morgan suggests that organizations are like organisms in terms of survival and adaption. Organizations and organisms live in "open" environments where information and resources flow freely. Over time, they inevitably move toward entropy, which is the tendency toward deterioration or death. The more a system is restricted from interacting with its environment, the more closed it becomes, thus driving a regression toward entropy.

Morgan explains that within open systems, organizations and organisms work interdependently against this entropy by seeking to remain in homeostasis, a state of regularity characterized by a continuous flow of information from the outside in, initiating activities to correct any deviations that may compromise the health of the system and assimilating deviations that may enrich it. In this way, organizations and organisms continue to evolve within an open system environment—sometimes experiencing challenges to their well-being but also being exposed to opportunities for enhancement.

Morgan's perspective supports the notion that welcoming the exchange of information and resources provided by strangers and by those with whom we have loose ties—in combination with those who are familiar—enhances the chances for survival through adaptation. Taking this theory further, we can see that the more people place themselves within environments that increase the possibilities of information transmission from multiple and diverse sources, the more occasion they will have to use this information productively.

The Coffeehouse Effect

A historic example of an environment that supports the open exchange of information is a coffeehouse, providing a public place where individuals from different cultures, professions, and economic strata collide. Steven Johnson calls these "liquid networks" where concepts can be repurposed and applied to multiple disciplines, thus sparking new ideas.[3] In his book *Where Good Ideas Come From*, Johnson shares the studies of Martin Ruef, a Stanford Business School professor who interviewed over 700 graduates to quantify the benefit of having access to large and diverse networks of people, as compared to those with more insular homogeneous social connections.

He discovered, through an analysis of their generation of new products and the number of trademarks and patents secured by these individuals, that those with the largest, most diverse social networks were "three times more innovative" than those who operated within smaller circles comprised of like-minded individuals—those within their own organizations.[4]

The value of a collaborative atmosphere to nurture a creative workplace has been demonstrated in a variety of contexts. In designing Pixar's headquarters, Steve Jobs understood the importance of where to put the bathrooms, café, mailboxes, and gift shop so that different people—different departments, organizations, economic strata—would unavoidably meet by chance, helping to convert strangers into people with loose ties, and thereby stimulating the exchange of information.[5]

Face-to-face interactions like those experienced in coffeehouses, and unexpectedly in bathrooms, are very different from electronic communications, which have become the ubiquitous form of interaction in the modern workplace. It is undeniable that the world, through social media innovations, has become more collaborative, but has this happened at the expense of our ability to connect in real time through in-person, face-to-face interactions that can teach us so much about the people in our proximity? Are we losing the skills needed to combine forces with acquaintances or strangers in person by relying on electronic media platforms to locate potential partners, make connections, and communicate?

In this increasingly digital landscape, "face time" matters more than ever as we find ourselves having fewer and fewer in-person exchanges. Why should we strive to preserve this type of communication in our daily lives? According to emotional intelligence expert Daniel Goleman, "Face-to-face interactions are information-rich; we pick up how to take what someone says to us not just from their tone of voice and facial expression, but also their body language, pacing, as well as their synchronization with what we do and say."[6] In one UCLA (University of California–Los Angeles) study, a group of sixth graders who spent five days away from digital screens (televisions, smartphones, and laptops) scored much higher at reading and responding to human emotions than those in the same class who stayed glued to their devices.[7] Have you ever said, "You're not at all like I imagined!" to someone you've communicated with only online after meeting him or her for the first time in person? This is because nonverbal cues allow us to connect and learn from each other in ways electronic communication simply cannot—a concept that has been well embraced by the business community.

In a survey of *Harvard Business Review* readers, 95 percent stated that face-to-face communication was essential to establishing and maintaining long-term relationships, and despite what others may think, these attitudes apply to millennials as well.[8] A University of Southern California study found that 80 percent of millennials surveyed worldwide identified face-to-face conversations as their preferred method for communicating with colleagues at work—rated higher than phone, e-mail, social media, and text messaging.[9] In many sectors, especially in the tech industry, work can be done almost exclusively from home, yet companies like Yahoo!, Microsoft, Pixar, and Google invest a great deal of money into creating collaborative workspaces so their employees can exchange information and ideas in person. Even smaller firms, such as Menlo Software Innovations in Ann Arbor, Michigan, have adopted a "bossless" office culture wherein employees report to one another and work side by side in large open spaces to spark creativity and innovation. Menlo highlights a "No one works alone" philosophy on its website and boasts an impressive client list that includes Pfizer, Domino's Pizza, and the University of Michigan.[10]

Leigh Harry, president of the International Congress and Convention Association (ICCA), believes face-to-face communication is key to "outside the box" thinking: "human interaction, especially face-to-face interaction, drives innovation and inspiration. Accidental connections between leading thinkers can unlock seemingly intractable challenges and insoluble puzzles."[11] This philosophy is not lost on Ben Waber, founder of Sociometric Solutions, a company that uses data to make offices more efficient. In a study he and his team conducted on Bank of America call centers across the country, the single largest predictor of employee success was the person's level of social engagement at work.[12] Essentially, the more employees interacted with their peers, the more their productivity and creativity spiked. Due to these findings, Bank of America went from staggering employee breaks throughout the day to suggesting groups take them together. This simple change resulted in teams that were more cohesive and innovative. Bank of America estimated that implementing similar policies across all its branches could save the company about $15 million a year.

However, while the benefits of face-to-face communication for enhancing productivity and innovation have been well established, studies show it also makes us happier. Researchers from Oregon Health & Science University found that an older person who has little in-person contact with others is twice as likely to develop depression two years later as compared to someone who is socially engaged; phone calls and e-mail, on the other hand, did not have the same positive effect.[13] In a social experiment conducted by behavioral scientists Nicholas Epley and Juliana Schroeder, 100 train commuters in Illinois were split into three groups.[14] Members of the first group were asked to strike up a conversation with other commuters, those in the second group were told to stay silent, and those in the third group carried on like they normally would. Riders then completed a survey rating how they felt after their commute. Those who initiated a conversation with strangers reported a much more pleasurable and productive experience than did those in the other two groups.

What is it about talking to strangers that not only makes us feel good, but sparks creativity and innovation? According to Steven Johnson, it has to do with what's referred to as "information spillover."[15] Progress didn't truly take off in our society until the rise of agriculture forced families wandering in small packs of hunter-gatherers to settle down in crowded spaces with complete strangers. The more one's network grew, the more good ideas could easily take hold, evolve, and grow. Johnson further explains that the best ideas occurred after the migration from "individual breakthroughs to the creative insights of the group."[16] The most powerful advances of the eighteenth century were in fact collaborative efforts of some of the greatest minds of the time contributing tweaks and improvements along the way. While history books often credit and praise the work of solo inventors, the reality is the industrial revolution was a direct result of what scholars refer to as "the collective wisdom."[17]

In his book *The Necessity of Strangers*, Alan Gregerman states that talking, engaging, learning, and collaborating with those we don't know is absolutely essential to individual growth and success.[18] He argues that strangers, more so than family and friends, are incredibly valuable precisely because of their differences—the knowledge and expertise they have that we don't have. Strangers have the ability to question, challenge, and be honest with us in ways those in our social circle cannot. Naturally, we gravitate toward friendships with people who are like us, and while good friends are often supportive and encouraging, that usually means they are agreeing with us when we may be better served by a different perspective. While we have been taught that success lies in "who you know," Gregerman believes true innovation and insight arise from those you don't know or, more importantly, those you could know. The average person has 150 friends, which makes up only 0.000000021 of the total population.[19] Imagine how limiting it is if one never reaches beyond that tiny network for new knowledge, ideas, or resources. According to Gregerman, the power of strangers lies in the following equation: "What I Already Know + My Knowledge or Understanding Gap + A Stranger (or Strangers) Who Knows How to Fill It = Business and Personal Success."[20]

This equation was proven in a study from the University of Pennsylvania's Wharton College of Business.[21] Researchers found that what gave companies the competitive edge was their ability to establish and take advantage of "performative ties"—impromptu knowledge exchanges between colleagues who don't know one another—no strings attached. Those who took the initiative to ask a stranger for business advice were able to reach a much higher level of success than their colleagues who were unwilling to go outside their usual networks. While many assume business success is dependent on friends helping friends, it was connecting with colleagues whom they had never met that made all the difference.

If we know that in-person interactions, especially with strangers, make us more creative, innovative, productive, and happy, why are we so hesitant to engage? According to Epley and Schroeder, it's because we are all operating under the false assumption that people don't want to talk to *us*.[22] We think others don't want to be bothered and turn inward into our comfort zones, even though many of us have a yearning to connect. In fact, many of the participants in Epley and Schroeder's study indicated that they would be more interested in talking than they thought their fellow commuters would be. This kind of thinking is referred to as pluralistic ignorance, when "people believe that others are less interested in connecting than they are themselves."[23] Have you ever put your earphones in or pretended to sleep on a plane to avoid conversations with strangers? When we all believe everyone would rather keep to themselves, breaking that barrier becomes even more terrifying and isolation becomes the accepted social norm.

There also is a stigma in our society associated with collaborative group work. Have you ever heard the expression, "If you want it done right, do it yourself"? Or listened to a room full of students groan after a group project was assigned? In academia, solo-authored research is given more weight than papers with multiple contributors, and we are conditioned at an early age to think working with others can hold us back or slow us down. We also have a difficult time coming from a disadvantaged place where others may know better than we do. Our first instinct is to defend or advocate for our positions, even when presented with conflicting evidence or ideas.

In her TED Talk "Connected but Alone?," MIT professor Sherry Turkle explains that face-to-face communication is much less comfortable because it doesn't allow us to present ourselves in the way we want to be seen.[24] Through e-mails, texts, and social media posts, we can carefully craft our words and control our actions, yet there are no rewrites or edits during an in-person conversation. Engaging with someone in real time means another person is seeing and responding to who we really are—uncensored. This explains why some relationships that originate online fall flat after face-to-face meetings. Many use technology to portray only the best versions of themselves, which eliminates a level of authenticity needed for meaningful connections.[25]

To address the many aversions people have to face-to-face conversations with strangers, the London-based organization Talk to Me Global planned a "Talk to Me London Day" that encouraged Londoners to engage in conversation with someone they didn't know, even if just for one day, while celebrating the value of talking to strangers.[26] The event evolved into a "Talk to Me" badge people could wear indicating they are open to having conversations with strangers. What the group found was that people often didn't know they wanted to talk to strangers until they experienced how good it could be. Therefore, they started organizing "first encounter" events that brought people together in controlled environments, giving them an excuse to connect. Such encounters included "The Big Lunch," where one day a year neighbors are encouraged to share a meal together; "Talk Bars," where people sit down in public places and order from a menu of conversation; and "Date While You Wait," where tables of board games are set up in places like subway stations where people are often waiting for long periods of time. The idea behind engineering first-encounter events is that these events then give people the excuse to follow up for a more natural "second encounter."[27]

In-person interactions with those we don't know expand our world and allow us to connect, learn, and grow in more significant ways. This in turn makes us happier, more inventive, and more creative. Our work and personal lives are enhanced as we become more insightful and compassionate. Yet, as technology plays a larger role in our lives, and we have fewer opportunities to interact in person, we forget how valuable these kinds of exchanges can be. The less we engage face-to-face, the harder it is to do, and fear and insecurity can create barriers that are difficult to break. Organizing first-encounter events that bring people (with a variety of experiences and backgrounds) together in low-pressure environments lets participants experience first-hand the many benefits of talking to strangers, and it gives others a reason to move forward with more meaningful second encounters. When people are connected with those they would never ordinarily meet and given the opportunity to really see one another, the possibilities for growth and innovation are endless.

NOTES

1. Karl Zinsmeister, "Oseola McCarty," The Philanthropy Roundtable, accessed October 11, 2016, www.philanthropyroundtable.org/almanac/hall_of_fame/oseola_mccarty.

2. Gareth Morgan, *Images of Organization*, Executive Edition (San Francisco: Berrett Koehler and Thousand Oaks, CA: SAGE, 1997), 40–42.

3. Steven Johnson, *Where Good Ideas Come From* (New York: Penguin, 2010), 43.

4. Ibid., 166.

5. Jonah Lehrer, "Steve Jobs: 'Technology Alone Is Not Enough,'" *The New Yorker*, News Desk, October 7, 2011, www.newyorker.com/news/news-desk/steve-jobs-technology-alone-is-not-enough.

6. Daniel Goleman, "Email with Care" (blog post), October 8, 2007, www.danielgoleman.info/email-with-care.

7. Yalda T. Uhls, Minas Michikyan, Jordan Morris, Debra Garcia, Gary W. Small, Eleni Zgourou, and Patricia M. Greenfield, "Five Days at Outdoor Education Camp without Screens Improves Preteen Skills with Nonverbal Emotion Cues," *Computers in Human Behavior* 39 (October 2014): 387–92.

8. Harvard Business Review Analytics Services, *Managing Across Distance in Today's Economic Climate: The Value of Face-to-Face Communication* (Harvard Business Review Analytic Services Report, Harvard Business School Publishing, 2009), https://hbr.org/resources/pdfs/comm/british-airways/hbras_ba_report_web.pdf.

9. News at Marshall, "Surprise! Millennials Prefer Face-to-Face not Facebook," Center for Effective Organizations, USC Marshall School of Business, October 15, 2013, www.marshall.usc.edu/news/releases/2013/surprise-millennials-prefer-face-face-not-facebook.

10. Elise Hu, "Inside the 'Bossless' Office, Where the Team Takes Charge," NPR, All Tech Considered, August 26, 2013, www.npr.org/sections/alltechconsidered/2013/08/27/207039346/What-Works-And-Doesnt-About-Bossless-Offices.

11. Lee Jago and Margaret Deery, *Delivering Innovation, Knowledge and Performance: The Role of Business Events* (Melbourne, Business Events Council of Australia, 2012), 12, www.businesseventscouncil.org.au/files/BE_Innov_Report_Mar10.pdf.

12. Ben Waber, *People Analytics: How Social Sensing Technology Will Transform Business and What It Tells Us about the Future of Work* (Upper Saddle River, NJ: FT Press, 2013), 77–87.

13. Alan R. Teo, Hwajung Choi, Sarah Beth Andrea, Marcia Valenstein, Jason T. Newsom, Steven Dobscha, and Kara Zivin, "Does Mode of Contact with Different Types of Social Relationships Predict Depression in Older Adults? Evidence from a Nationally Representative Survey," *Journal of the American Geriatrics Society* 63, no. 10 (October 2015): 2014–22.

14. Nicholas Epley and Juliana Schroeder, "Mistakenly Seeking Solitude," *Journal of Experimental Psychology* 143 (October 2014): 1980–99.

15. Johnson, *Where Good Ideas Come From*, 53.

16. Ibid.

17. Ibid.

18. Alan Gregerman, *The Necessity of Strangers* (San Francisco: Jossey-Bass, 2013).

19. Ibid., 12–13.

20. Ibid., 17.

21. Sheen Sha'hal Levine, "The Strength of Performative Ties: Three Essays on Knowledge, Social Networks, and Exchange" (Dissertation, University of Pennsylvania, January 1, 2005), http://repository.upenn.edu/dissertations/AAI3197702.

22. Epley and Schroeder, "Mistakenly Seeking Solitude."

23. Ibid., 1986.

24. Sherry Turkle, "Connected, but Alone?," TED Talk, February 2012, www.ted.com/talks/sherry_turkle_alone_together.

25. Ibid.

26. Talk to Me Global, *It's Good to Talk: Overcoming the Barriers That Stop Us Talking to Strangers* (Executive report, 2016), http://talktome.global/images/Its_Good_to_Talk_Report.pdf.

27. Ibid.

Introduction to CoLAB Workshops

Knowing the importance of interacting with strangers and accepting the indispensable role of face-to-face conversations in forming capable partnerships—especially in academic and nonprofit sectors where collaborative project-based activities increasingly are the norm—the question then becomes this: How can people in these environments most effectively combine forces to generate ideas for contributing to projects, initiating new projects, or accessing invisible resources that accelerate these efforts? CoLAB Workshops offer structured group activities to do just that. This chapter defines the CoLAB Planning Series and provides the backstory of its development. It also offers two workshop visualizations, one for individuals and one for organization representatives.

What Is a CoLAB Workshop?

Along with sharing insights about the various ways in which people work together, and about methods for developing creativity, the CoLAB's specific purposes are to (1) facilitate the discovery of hidden resources and/or potential partnership relationships; (2) generate new ideas for innovation and research; and (3) advance the resolution of problematic situations by leveraging extant yet untapped assets. CoLABs create a structured, engaging, and welcoming "café" environment where workshop participants can connect to strangers and/or their colleagues to discover hidden commonalities, diversities, expertise, resources, networks, and creative opportunities. One important distinction of CoLAB Workshops is that they are not intended to be networking sessions in the traditional sense. No one is selling anything—not themselves, their projects, or their ideas.

The essential character of a CoLAB can be compared to the experience of spending an afternoon with other coffee drinkers in a British café during the Age of Enlightenment or an evening at a Parisian bar during the Age of Impressionism (think: Woody Allen's film *Midnight in Paris*). Steven Johnson, a science innovation researcher, posits that the stimulant coffee sold in European seventeenth-century coffeehouses created a culture, a hub, an information network of the time, where café goers met strangers and colleagues from multiple disciplines and with diverse knowledge who shared ideas and leveraged existing assets that were crucial to fueling innovation.[1] For instance, Johnson recounts that the concept of the "modern insurance industry came into being at Lloyd's of London, a portside coffeehouse where ship captains would meet and end up sharing ideas about ways to decrease risk in shipping."[2]

In contrast to today's typical one-person-speaks-at-a-time meetings or presentations, CoLABs offer a fertile atmosphere where interesting topics can be discussed by everyone simultaneously in the room while also learning about the hidden assets "owned" by others. The connections made in these environments provide a variety of benefits during the workshop itself, and more importantly, they can form the foundation for initiating short- or long-term partnerships through postworkshop conversations. CoLAB processes unlock human potential concealed within any given gathering of strangers in real time. They serve to convene a group of individuals, each seeking out others who may contribute in some way to actualize future dreams, programs, projects, or ideas that will ultimately change people's lives. An African proverb helps to describe the intent of CoLAB processes: "If you want to go fast, go alone; if you want to go far, go together." "Going together" isn't always easy, especially when you don't know whom to go with. Participant feedback supports the notion that CoLAB-facilitated processes may well be the very best way to quickly and enthusiastically initiate collaborative relationships with new stakeholders. (For more information about CoLAB results, see chapter 3.)

The CoLAB Planning Series is a set of facilitated group activities and processes designed for a minimum of 14 individuals and up to more than 120 that can be customized to last from 1.5 hours to up to 12 hours. The workshop sessions focus on revealing the assets of participants, many of which will have been unknown to most, if not all, of those attending. CoLAB Workshops serve two major types of participants: those representing their individual professional or scholastic interests (workshops for individuals) and those representing another entity, which could be a library, museum, or other nonprofit or governmental organization where they are employed or in which they are a member or serve as a volunteer (workshops for organizations).

The centerpiece of every CoLAB Workshop is the facilitation of one-on-one "speed-meetings" where each participant—in the case of workshops for individuals—quickly reveals his or her own professional interests, passions, skills, resources, and other assets; or where participants share information about their organizations' programs and operations and the populations they serve. (See figure 2.1.) The sharing of this information occurs during structured rounds of three- to four-minute conversations in which participants pair off and talk together on any topic they choose.

Through postworkshop feedback, presenters have found that most of the information shared during CoLABs may otherwise have remained a mystery to workshop participants had they not attended the workshop. These workshops greatly reduce the time it takes to open the door to information that others have access to, whether within their own geographic community or—in the case of a classroom or conference CoLAB—within their discipline. New relationships and information generated during CoLABs enable access to resources and methods for improving community situations or for enhancing existing projects or programs.

FIGURE 2.1

UNIVERSITY OF FLORIDA COLLEGE OF THE ARTS FACULTY CoLAB

Photo by Barbara Hood

What Happens during CoLAB Workshops?

The best way to understand what happens during a CoLAB is, of course, to attend a workshop. As an alternative, the following visualizations of actual CoLAB Workshops, one for individuals and one for organization representatives, provide concrete descriptions of the activities that make up a CoLAB. These visualizations may help you to create your own mental movie of CoLAB Workshops.

Visualization 1: CoLAB Workshop for Individuals: Collaborating with Strangers on Sustainability Projects at the University of Florida

This workshop was attended by eighty-four participants (see figure 2.2), about thirty of whom were undergraduates in courses related to the topic of sustainability, and the others were graduate students, faculty, or administrators interested in the topic. The workshop was scheduled for a weekday from 1:00 to 3:00 p.m. in the George A. Smathers Libraries' large multipurpose presentation room, which holds up to 300 people. Participants randomly began arriving at 12:45 p.m., and each was provided with a marker, a name tag with his or her participant number, and a blank profile-sign with space to

FIGURE 2.2

POSTCARD PROMOTING SUSTAINABILITY CoLAB AT UNIVERSITY OF FLORIDA

Design by Barbara Hood

answer five questions. Participants were oriented quickly by greeters who requested that they (1) find a seat at one of the tables to complete the information requested on their profile-signs and (2) have their headshot photo taken against a blank wall near the registration area. Participants were told that the workshop would begin when most had completed these two activities. Greeters also pointed out the available cookies, bottled water, and boxed juices.

A few days prior to the workshop, registrants had received an e-mail message requesting that they familiarize themselves with the five profile questions and think about formulating answers to these questions in preparation for the workshop. Figure 2.3 shows an example of one of the completed profile-signs from that workshop.

By 1:20, most registrants had arrived and had either completed or nearly completed their profile-signs, and all had had their headshots taken. The lead facilitator welcomed participants and encouraged those who were still preparing their profile-signs to continue working on them during the twenty-minute PowerPoint presentation, which provided a brief history of CoLABs; an orientation as to the workshop goals along with a short video excerpt of Steven Johnson's TED Talk "Where Good Ideas Come From"[3] an introduction to the basic principles of asset-based collaboration; descriptions of ways in which to partner with others; recommendations for activities that enhance one's

FIGURE 2.3

PARTICIPANT PROFILE-SIGN AT THE SUSTAINABILITY CoLAB

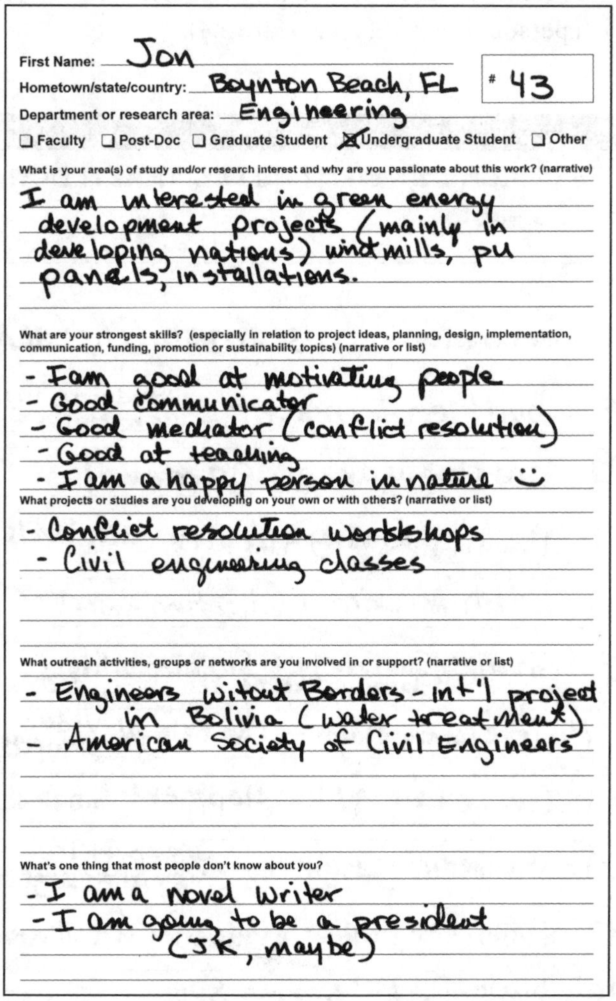

First Name: **Jon**

Hometown/state/country: **Boynton Beach, FL** **# 43**

Department or research area: **Engineering**

☐ Faculty ☐ Post-Doc ☐ Graduate Student ☒ Undergraduate Student ☐ Other

What is your area(s) of study and/or research interest and why are you passionate about this work? (narrative)

I am interested in green energy development projects (mainly in developing nations) windmills, pu panels, installations.

What are your strongest skills? (especially in relation to project ideas, planning, design, implementation, communication, funding, promotion or sustainability topics) (narrative or list)

- I am good at motivating people
- Good communicator
- Good mediator (conflict resolution)
- Good at teaching
- I am a happy person in nature ☺

What projects or studies are you developing on your own or with others? (narrative or list)

- Conflict resolution workshops
- Civil engineering classes

What outreach activities, groups or networks are you involved in or support? (narrative or list)

- Engineers witout Borders - int'l project in Bolivia (water treatment)
- American Society of Civil Engineers

What's one thing that most people don't know about you?

- I am a novel writer
- I am going to be a president (JK, maybe)

creativity; and instructions for participating in the speed-meeting process that directly followed the presentation. (For more information about slide content, see chapter 4, Scenario 1, Step 13.)

At the slide featuring instructions for the speed-meetings, the facilitator reviewed each step, providing additional context for activities that might be more challenging than others. The following instructions were reviewed:

1. Find a participant you do not know.
2. Locate/check the participant's number on your checklist so you will remember with whom you spoke.
3. Read your partner's sign.
4. Converse for three minutes about whatever topic you want to discuss.
5. You may sit or stand or move to a quiet area.
6. Listen for instructions throughout the session.
7. When you hear the bell, say good-bye and find a new stranger.
8. Take notes—no need to capture contact information.

In the next step, the facilitator invited participants to affix their profile-signs to their chests using the safety pin attached to each sign. She explained that this gives participants the hands-free ability to take notes so they can recall the conversation and note the number of each person they meet (see figure 2.4).

PARTICIPANT'S CHECKLIST WITH NOTES TAKEN DURING SPEED-MEETINGS

At this point (1:45 p.m.), everyone was prepared for their speed-meeting interactions and the process began. For the next hour and ten minutes, participants were able to meet and engage in seventeen, three-minute, one-on-one conversations. At first, the volume of conversations was quite low, as participants got used to the routine of finding a partner, reading each other's profile-signs, and then talking about whatever came to mind. After the third round of speed-meetings, the volume began growing and the quickness in which participants were finding new partners accelerated. The energy in the room was palpable. By the tenth meeting, the atmosphere more resembled a party than a workshop. (See figure 2.5.)

FIGURE 2.5

SPEED-MEETINGS DURING THE SUSTAINABILITY CoLAB

Photo by Barbara Hood

Although most of the rounds were smooth sailing, there also were many "redirections of traffic" during this workshop with eighty-four participants. Facilitators helped to redirect those who didn't decouple in time for the new round by interrupting other participants who had engaged in their next speed-meeting round to integrate the late decouplers.

After seventeen rounds the last bell was rung, participants were asked to sit down, remove their profile-signs, and write answers to the following three questions: What synergies or connections did you discover? What did you learn? What are your next steps? Participants spent ten minutes writing answers on Post-it notes, and facilitators helped affix their Post-its to the three Idea Boards located at the front of the room. Some participants spent a few moments reading what others had written.

The last instruction was for participants to complete the contact information, the permissions form for using photographs online or for other promotional purposes, and an evaluation survey located on the back side of the profile-sign to reflect on their workshop experience (see chapter 3). A few participants preferred not to have their headshot photo loaded to the CoLAB website and noted that preference on their profile-sign. A CoLAB team member took group photographs of all the workshop activities for posting to the website. Collecting all of the supplies and profile-signs brought the workshop to a conclusion at the end of two hours.

Following the workshop, CoLAB project team members uploaded headshots, contact information, and scans of profile-signs to the Collaborating with Strangers website (www.uflib.ufl.edu/communications/colab/home.html). A password-protected link allowed for postworkshop follow-up browsing of headshots and profile-signs, inspiring future interactions.

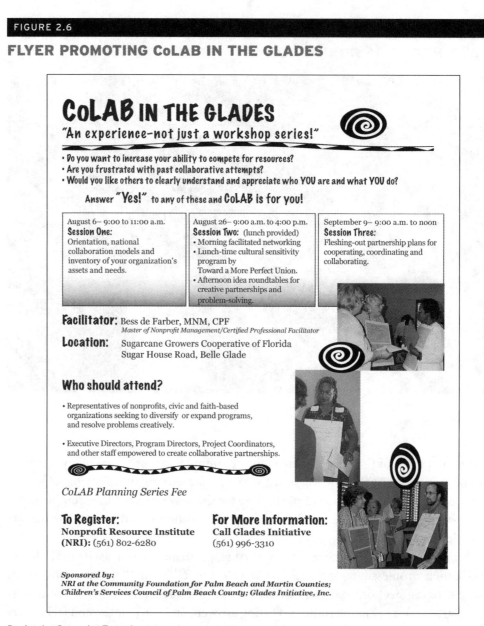

FIGURE 2.6

FLYER PROMOTING CoLAB IN THE GLADES

CoLAB IN THE GLADES
"An experience–not just a workshop series!"

• Do you want to increase your ability to compete for resources?
• Are you frustrated with past collaborative attempts?
• Would you like others to clearly understand and appreciate who YOU are and what YOU do?

Answer "Yes!" to any of these and CoLAB is for you!

| August 6– 9:00 to 11:00 a.m. **Session One:** Orientation, national collaboration models and inventory of your organization's assets and needs. | August 26– 9:00 a.m. to 4:00 p.m. **Session Two:** (lunch provided) • Morning facilitated networking • Lunch-time cultural sensitivity program by Toward a More Perfect Union. • Afternoon idea roundtables for creative partnerships and problem-solving. | September 9– 9:00 a.m. to noon **Session Three:** Fleshing-out partnership plans for cooperating, coordinating and collaborating. |

Facilitator: Bess de Farber, MNM, CPF
Master of Nonprofit Management/Certified Professional Facilitator

Location: Sugarcane Growers Cooperative of Florida
Sugar House Road, Belle Glade

Who should attend?

• Representatives of nonprofits, civic and faith-based organizations seeking to diversify or expand programs, and resolve problems creatively.

• Executive Directors, Program Directors, Project Coordinators, and other staff empowered to create collaborative partnerships.

CoLAB Planning Series Fee

To Register:
**Nonprofit Resource Institute
(NRI):** (561) 802-6280

For More Information:
Call Glades Initiative
(561) 996-3310

Sponsored by:
NRI at the Community Foundation for Palm Beach and Martin Counties;
Children's Services Council of Palm Beach County; Glades Initiative, Inc.

Design by Casandra Tanenbaum

Visualization 2: CoLAB Workshop for Organization Representatives in the Glades

Similar to the two-hour Collaborating with Strangers on Sustainability Projects at UF, the Glades CoLAB attracted a large and diverse contingent of participants, this time comprised of representatives from nonprofit organizations and groups (some organizations sent two representatives) working in Palm Beach County. (See figure 2.6.)

In preparing for this three-day, twelve-hour-long workshop, facilitators divided the organizations represented (alphabetically by name of organization) into two equal groups. One group would be represented by yellow profile-signs, and the other group would use blue profile-signs. A checklist of all participating organizations was provided

FIGURE 2.7

ORGANIZATION REPRESENTATIVE CHECKLIST EXAMPLE

Checklist

	Yellow Profile Signs	Comments
☐	AIDS Awareness Poets	
☐	Alzheimer's Community Care	
☐	City of Belle Glade Community Development	
☐	Delray Beach Poetry Slam (Poets Anonymous)	
☐	Glades Health Care Center	
☐	Glades Initiative	
☐	Gulfstream Goodwill Industries	
☐	HEART Health Education Advocators Resources Team Inc.	

to all participants to help them keep track of speed-meeting partners during each round (see figure 2.7).

The workshop was held in a large room with folding chairs and long folding tables at the headquarters of a major corporation in Belle Glade, Florida, which was the only suitable space available in this small remote town. Session one, held from 9:00 to 11:00 a.m., provided an orientation to impart information about various collaboration methods; to relate stories of exemplary collaborative initiatives and dynamic organizational leaders; to share asset-based community development strategies; and to complete a large group activity for discovering the various types of facilities, skills, and resources accessible to those attending. The session concluded with the completion of survey forms that provided information about each organization's mission, programs, facilities, volunteers, partnerships, and funding sources to be used at the next session (see figure 2.8).

FIGURE 2.8

SESSION I: CoLAB PLANNING SERIES PARTICIPANT PROFILE AND INVENTORY

Due by 5:00 p.m. on Tuesday, August 17th

E-mail: _____ Fax: _____

Contact Bess de Farber to confirm receipt and ask questions.

GENERAL INFORMATION

Organization

Participant/Name and Title

E-mail   Phone   Fax

How long with this organization?

Previous nonprofit work?

Mission (No more than 15 words)

Geographic Area Served: Circle: West   North   South   Central   All

Be specific in terms of city (cities):

Administrative Office Location(s)/Hours of Operation

Program Site Location(s)/Hours of Operation

Describe Clients (elderly, special needs, K-12, etc.)

ORGANIZATIONAL ASSETS

Staff (How many?)   Volunteers (How many?)

Programs (list):

How many clients served in each program?

Total clients served last year?

Organizational Capabilities? (marketing, special events, donor development, members, etc.)

Staff/Volunteer Special Skills?

Current Partnerships/Collaborations

ORGANIZATIONAL NEEDS

For session two, 9:00 a.m. to 4:00 p.m. on the second day (including lunch), participants arrived to find their survey information transformed into yellow and blue profile-signs. The room was lined along the walls with these signs. After providing instructions about the speed-meeting process, representatives were instructed to retrieve their profile-signs, tie them around their necks using the ribbon provided, and begin the process by finding a partner of the same sign color for the first set of speed-meetings. Speed-meetings continued, round by round, until everyone had met each of those within their own sign-color group. Facilitators rang bells to signal the end of each speed-meeting round. After lunch, the instruction to participants was to find a partner, in each round, whose profile-sign was a different color from their own. This activity consumed most of the day. Each participant engaged in a total of thirty-one three-minute, speed-meeting conversations. The final activity of session two was for participants to reflect on their speed-meetings and to make a list of all the organization representatives with whom they planned to follow up, along with ideas that they wanted to pursue with each organization they listed (see figure 2.9).

FIGURE 2.9

POTENTIAL PARTNERSHIPS IDENTIFIED AFTER SPEED-MEETINGS BY A NONPROFIT ORGANIZATION REPRESENTATIVE IN THE GLADES

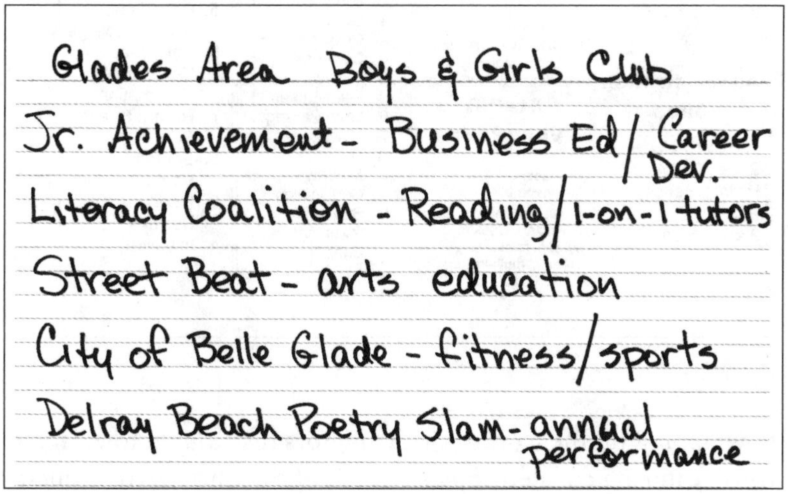

Glades Area Boys & Girls Club
Jr. Achievement - Business Ed/Career Dev.
Literacy Coalition - Reading/1-on-1 tutors
Street Beat - arts education
City of Belle Glade - fitness/sports
Delray Beach Poetry Slam - annual performance

During session three, held on the third day from 9:00 a.m. to 12:00 p.m., participants viewed a presentation illuminating all of the ideas each organization had generated during session two. Organizations were divided into groups for hosting small-group discussions to brainstorm questions about how best to access or contribute to one another's programs, facilities, and other assets. An evaluation survey was distributed and completed by participants, some of whom were so happy with their profile-signs that they carried them off with them as they left. (See figure 2.10.)

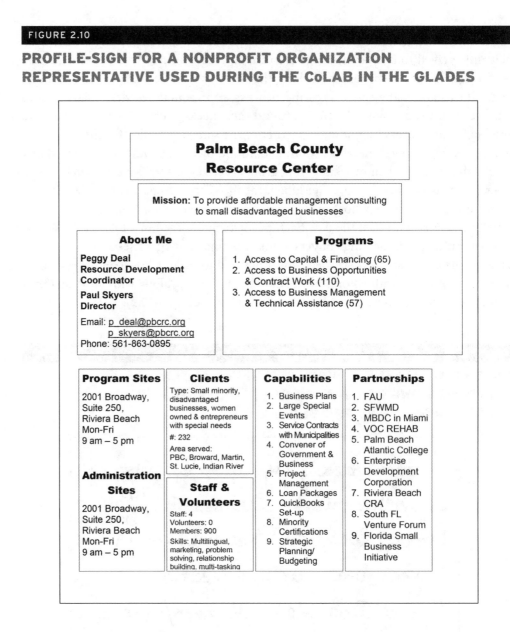

FIGURE 2.10

PROFILE-SIGN FOR A NONPROFIT ORGANIZATION REPRESENTATIVE USED DURING THE CoLAB IN THE GLADES

Palm Beach County Resource Center

Mission: To provide affordable management consulting to small disadvantaged businesses

About Me

Peggy Deal
Resource Development
Coordinator

Paul Skyers
Director

Email: p_deal@pbcrc.org
p_skyers@pbcrc.org
Phone: 561-863-0895

Programs

1. Access to Capital & Financing (65)
2. Access to Business Opportunities & Contract Work (110)
3. Access to Business Management & Technical Assistance (57)

Program Sites

2001 Broadway,
Suite 250,
Riviera Beach
Mon-Fri
9 am – 5 pm

Administration Sites

2001 Broadway,
Suite 250,
Riviera Beach
Mon-Fri
9 am – 5 pm

Clients

Type: Small minority, disadvantaged businesses, women owned & entrepreneurs with special needs
#: 232
Area served:
PBC, Broward, Martin, St. Lucie, Indian River

Staff & Volunteers

Staff: 4
Volunteers: 0
Members: 900
Skills: Multilingual, marketing, problem solving, relationship building, multi-tasking

Capabilities

1. Business Plans
2. Large Special Events
3. Service Contracts with Municipalities
4. Convener of Government & Business
5. Project Management
6. Loan Packages
7. QuickBooks Set-up
8. Minority Certifications
9. Strategic Planning/ Budgeting

Partnerships

1. FAU
2. SFWMD
3. MBDC in Miami
4. VOC REHAB
5. Palm Beach Atlantic College
6. Enterprise Development Corporation
7. Riviera Beach CRA
8. South FL Venture Forum
9. Florida Small Business Initiative

Prior to wrapping up the workshop, facilitators distributed to each participant a *Book of Signs*, featuring collated copies of each of the thirty-two profile-signs along with participant names and contact information.

Origin and History of CoLAB Workshops

In 1997, co-author Bess de Farber, was working as a nonprofit management consultant specializing in grants management consulting and training. She received a request from the Community Foundation of Broward, in Broward County, Florida, to deliver a training session on the topic of collaboration development. In the 1990s, when collaborative activities were emerging more visibly in the nonprofit sector, philanthropic organizations began establishing policies for grant applicants that encouraged the inclusion of collaborative partnerships within their grant proposals. At the time, most organization leaders and staff members had little formal training related to best practices or theories of how to partner with other organizations in the development of plans and programs for improving efficiencies, reducing duplication of effort, and, most importantly, increasing the number of constituents who would benefit from programs and services provided by nonprofit organizations.

De Farber's approach to this training opportunity became a test case, experimenting with activities she had never before facilitated. Her strategy was to share the basic theories of ways in which organizations actually partnered with each other, based on literature produced by the Amherst H. Wilder Foundation as a result of its staff's research on the topic of collaboration within and among nonprofit organizations.[4] In order to effectively define the term "collaboration," Wilder Foundation researchers found it necessary to include definitions related to "cooperation" and to "coordination." As de Farber explains:

> Another significant modality in which people also have opportunities to combine forces is through mentoring relationships. . . . Moving from cooperating to coordinating, and finally to collaborating is a progression involving increases in the level of effort, interdependence, and risk among those individuals and organizations seeking to work with each other. Beginning with cooperation, the researchers surmised that this category was the simplest and least intrusive. It involves no risk for either party but requires some minimal level of communication. During cooperative activities, both of the participating individuals or entities retain their separateness in the use of their own resources, and in resulting benefits received from the cooperative effort. . . . This is a very passive, informal way to share resources.
>
> The second mode in which organizations work together is to coordinate. Coordinating with external organizations requires more communication, planning, and effort among participating entities, and can pose greater risks . . . available resources are likely more abundant and benefits tend to be more mutually recognized.
>
> Collaboration is the third and most challenging way in which organizations and individuals combine forces, possibly because of the many risks these types of projects and programs usually present. This type of working relationship is distinguishable based on the activities that require extensive planning; defined communication roles and channels; and contributions of resources from both entities that are usually combined and shared in new ways. The commitment to work in this new structure usually comes from a common mission or purpose to solve a problem, fill a gap, or to take advantage of the leveraging of extant resources to create something new and valuable.[5]

Another key component of de Farber's 1997 agenda for the Introduction to Collaboration workshop experiment was the inclusion of the work of John P. Kretzmann and John L. McKnight, two Northwestern University professors in the Center for Urban Affairs and Policy Research, who had published a guide to rebuilding "troubled communities," *Building Communities from the Inside Out.*[6] Kretzmann and McKnight set out to establish step-by-step guidelines for creating an inventory of the assets otherwise hidden within communities by employing the strategy they termed "asset-based community development." Their intent was to strengthen communities by discovering a given community's incalculable and diverse assets and then accessing these assets to improve communities. The alternative needs-based model relies largely on seeking external resources and funding to fill the gaps identified by a community's assessed needs.

During the actual workshop, de Farber followed her agenda to share these key concepts with the seventeen participants, who represented a variety of nonprofit organization types. One activity was to share a list of their organizations' assets with others in four small groups of four or five people. Then, simply to move toward applicability of these concepts, de Farber instructed participants in the four groups to spend twenty minutes brainstorming a new project that would combine each group's available assets to produce a positive result that would improve other people's lives. During the debriefing of this activity, participants were surprised to discover that out of the four small groups, three had developed viable new projects that combined assets from each small-group participant, and that within each of the three successful collaborating groups, a philanthropic organization representative was interested in discussing the possible financial support of these three new projects. The success of this stand-alone workshop proved, both to de Farber and also to those who had just experienced the unexpected results, that focusing on accessible assets and combining them in new ways can be a very effective collaboration tool for community members, one requiring only a small investment of their time.

In a subsequent request from the director of the Community Foundation of Broward's Nonprofit Resource Center (NRC) to design a more intensive collaboration training workshop, the opportunity to experiment further with these concepts became available. It was November of 2001, and in Broward County, as well as across the nation, the events of 9/11 were rocking the nonprofit community. Charitable gifts, which had previously supported a wide range of causes, were now increasingly being channeled to causes more narrowly associated with 9/11. This, in conjunction with a significant decline in the stock market during that time, created a situation of scarcity within the philanthropic giving community. Because funding was becoming more difficult to acquire, competition between organizations intensified, and many small organizations serving minority communities suffered the most. In an effort to remediate this competitive atmosphere and foster a sense of community, de Farber, under the auspices of the NRC, convened several community representatives from the United Way, National Conference for Community and Justice, ArtServe, Cultural Council, and the NRC to outline the new activities and group processes for a proposed intensive two-day workshop that would initiate a planning process and create organization partnerships in real time. With their strong endorsement, de Farber set out to develop and present the first CoLAB Planning Workshop.

To design this inaugural two-day CoLAB, de Farber drew on her past experiences as program officer for a cultural council and also for a community foundation overseeing the submissions, review, and grants management activities of awards to organizations in the categories of tourism, arts and culture, social services, and human and race relations. She also had served as a review panelist for such organizations as the National Endowment for the Arts and the Florida Division of Cultural Affairs. In reading hundreds of proposals over several years, it became evident that applicants were missing valuable opportunities to partner with each other on their proposed programs and projects. Many proposals she reviewed were prepared without drawing on the diverse expertise and other more tangible assets available within the communities, which would have added value and exciting innovative possibilities to these proposals. But as a program officer and review panelist, her role prevented her from playing matchmaker after proposals had been submitted. She recognized that this new workshop presented an opportunity to address the barriers preventing viable collaborative partnerships from forming.

De Farber also determined that adequately mapping assets, as advocated by Kretzmann and McKnight,[7] should be a central component of this workshop. The process of inventorying a community to discern its available and diverse assets, however, could be daunting and slow, consuming hundreds of hours and a small army of interviewers. In analyzing the laborious inventorying requirement, de Farber pondered whether an alternative method could be used to more quickly access key information about community and organizational assets. If this could be possible in a workshop setting, representatives of participating organizations would easily and naturally be able to generate new ideas for ways in which they could combine assets to work together.

The question then became this: How can the activities during a two-day workshop facilitate the initiation of cooperative, coordinative, collaborative or mentoring relationships when convening a large number of nonprofit organization representatives? The resulting answer has become the cornerstone of all CoLAB Workshops: the use of a profile-sign, worn or held by each participant, that reveals information about each participant's assets during one-on-one speed-meetings. These signs eliminated the need for lengthy surveying methods to create a viable asset inventory.

The inaugural two-day CoLAB Planning Series Workshop was held in 2002 at the Community Foundation for Palm Beach and Martin Counties, whose staff was ready to experiment with the presentation of such an unusual intensive workshop. The success of the Palm Beach and Martin County CoLAB became evident in the energy and commitment of the forty-eight organization representatives who invested their precious work time during this thirteen-hour workshop. In fact, at its conclusion, most of the participants didn't want to leave and remained conversing while facilitators straightened up the room and packed up supplies. (The CoLAB Workshop that was initially planned for Broward County was subsequently presented in 2003.)

At the time of this writing, approximately 600 organizations and over 2,000 individuals have participated in CoLAB Workshops. Workshops varying in length and attended by 14 to 120 participants have been sponsored and/or hosted by nine nonprofit and philanthropic organizations, four government agencies, two corporations, five conferences, and sixteen academic units within five institutions of higher education.

Since 2002, modifications to the workshops have been implemented to maximize benefits. For instance, at the University of Florida (UF), facilitators considered the needs of students and faculty to access supplementary postworkshop resources. Adding participant headshots to accompany workshop profile-signs—using a password-protected webpage—increased the ease by which browsing could occur and connections could be made. It also allowed for UF CoLAB participants to view the profiles and headshots from other workshops they had not attended.

Strategies for Designing Effective Profile-Signs

For every workshop, facilitators have customized the profile-sign questions or the survey forms for gathering information about organizations whose representatives have registered to attend. The quality of information shared by participants is directly related to the degree of workshop success. For instance, for individual participants in a classroom setting or academic institution who are simply representing their own professional or academic interests, use of the following questions has proved to be most beneficial:

1. *What is your area of study or research interest and why are you passionate about this work?* This question is important in that it gets to the heart of a participant's interests. In a few sentences, or by using a bulleted list, the participant can share information about his or her current research project, discipline of study, professional career, or any number of other topics of sincere interest. During a speed-meeting, pairs may be acquainted with each other somehow or they may never have met or seen their partners prior to attending the CoLAB. Regardless, this question will reveal unique information about a participant that is likely to be new to their CoLAB speed-meeting partners. It is a question that typically we do not ask our colleagues or the strangers with whom we come in contact.

2. *What are your strongest skills?* This is another question we avoid asking others, unless it is part of a job interview process. Again, however, it provides key information about assets available to the profile owner that otherwise most likely would remain hidden during the workshop. If you were attending this type of partnership-inspiring workshop, wouldn't you want to know what skills others might have that could contribute to your own extant skills—skills accessible to your partner that you may be able to acquire through some sort of mentoring relationship, or that the profile owner may be able to offer to enhance or actualize a project that you are currently developing?

3. *What projects or studies are you developing on your own or with others?* Here is an opportunity for the profile owner to provide a window into his or her most recent or significant collaborative activities. This information can paint a quick picture during speed-meeting rounds about the work to which this profile owner has contributed.

4. *What outreach activities, groups, or networks are you involved in or do you support?* Here, too, this question reveals where the profile owner has chosen to invest his or her time, whether professionally or personally, and as a result, this information can be invaluable to increase a workshop partner's understanding about the profile owner's values and priorities. It also shares information about others whom the profile owner can access for networking, for brainstorming solutions related to a project, or for inspiring a partner to become otherwise involved.

5. *What is one thing most people don't know about you?* This question has become the most popular of those included on the profile-signs of individual participants. It can reveal a profile owner's most hidden assets. Consider these answers that have appeared on profile-signs: "I'm a triplet." "I played in two world bagpiping championships." "I own a house in Rwanda." No matter what the

answer, it is usually unique and opens up a whole new avenue of conversation and improbable connections. If, for instance, partners have trouble imagining a topic to engage in (during a three- to four-minute conversation after reading the previous answers), then the answer to this question can suddenly take the pair in a completely different direction.

In conjunction with the theme of this last question, facilitators also have asked individual participants to provide some basic information about themselves, such as their hometowns. This can be answered with whatever name the profile owner feels is his or her hometown, not necessarily where he or she was born or raised. The profile owner's answer gives workshop partners context about him or her that is otherwise inaccessible. It can provide an easy entry into a stranger's life and a key topic of conversation during the speed-meeting rounds.

Profile questions designed for participants who are attending on behalf of organizations are often conveyed through a survey instrument after a representative has registered for a workshop. The goal of the survey is to discern sufficiently and quickly the nature of an organization's mission, size, community impact, and resources so that a workshop partner can explore connections while learning as much as possible about the organization during the thirty seconds it takes to review a profile-sign. The CoLAB organization workshop survey typically asks these questions:

- What is the organization's mission?
- What programs does it provide?
- How many people are served by each program?
- What facilities and locations does your organization use to provide programs?
- What are the organization's hours of operation and services?
- How many staff members are employed by the organization?
- How many volunteers support the organization annually?
- What are the organization's primary funding sources?

You will notice that these questions, like those elicited from individual participants, are factual and reveal a variety of asset types. But there are some questions that should never be asked on a profile-sign for either individuals or organizations. Take, for instance, a question regarding a profile owner's opinions, say about politics, his or her work environment and colleagues, or an issue troubling a community. Answers to such questions are debatable and potentially could be harmful to the goal of initiating collaborative relationships that leverage untapped assets.

Other profile-sign questions to avoid include those which focus on problem identification, needs, or deficits. By including these types of questions, participants run the risk of focusing on what is unavailable and even impossible. Needs-based planning methods for solving community problems typically rely on the acquisition of funding that often is out of reach. This approach takes longer to show progress, doesn't necessarily broaden participation, and can foster a sense of pessimism. Needs-based planning also can lead to doubting the feasibility of an idea or a project that otherwise would be viable had those considering the project or idea taken an asset-based approach. Any question that doesn't reveal information about assets should be considered inappropriate for a CoLAB Workshop profile-sign.

Basic Principles and Conditions That Yield the Best Results

Beyond the protocols described earlier for designing profile-signs, CoLAB Workshops operate best under these conditions, which together form the CoLAB guiding principles: (1) voluntary participation, (2) local geographic focus, (3) the practice of face-to-face conversations with others known and unknown, (4) a mixture of diverse disciplines, (5) multiple conversations within a short period of time, and (6) an understanding that this information discovery process may or may not yield immediate and/or long-term applicable results.

1. *Participants should self-select to attend.* This is the underlying condition on which all others are dependent. It ensures that the CoLAB experience will be an enjoyable one for every participant. There have been a few instances during past CoLABs where one person in attendance clearly did not self-select to attend and was not happy about participating. Mandated participation by only one participant in a workshop can taint the experience for each partner participant that the "representative" meets. And a disgruntled participant is less likely either to enjoy or to benefit much from the experience.

    Unfortunately, this can happen for a few students in a classroom whose teacher is hosting a CoLAB Workshop for the purpose of forming assignment project teams. Because none of the students can opt out, some of the students may feel "forced" to participate. In these situations, the majority of students will engage wholeheartedly in the process and, in turn, will reap the many rewards from those they meet with. But there can be a few who resent being forced to speak one-on-one to others in the class. It's an unavoidable risk when CoLABs are facilitated within a class unless an opt-out alternative is offered.

2. *CoLAB Workshops are most effective when locally based and centered on a singular theme or community issue.* Having conversations with people who all work or reside within a one-hour commute radius allows for the possibility of more frequent contact, more in-depth knowledge of community assets, and a higher potential for creatively leveraging these assets. By adding a theme or topic such as literacy, the assets and information shared during the workshop become more focused, which in turn allows resources, expertise, and knowledge to be more rapidly explored.

    When a CoLAB is presented at a conference attracting participants from different parts of the country or from multiple countries, it can be effective in creating a sense of community within a conference; however, the lack of proximity of those participating can reduce the potential future benefits experienced compared to when all participants reside and work in the same geographical area.

3. *CoLAB Workshops set the stage for practicing face-to-face communication to initiate relationships in real time, without the assistance of technology.* Developing and practicing interpersonal communication skills have become imperative. Dr. Gary Small, a UCLA neuroscientist, studies the evolutionary changes being detected in the next tech-savvy generation as they "neglect human contact skills and lose the ability to read emotional expressions and body language."[8]

He continues, "The people in the next generation who are really going to have the edge are the ones who master the technological skills and also face-to-face skills. They will know when the best response to an email or instant message is to talk rather than sit and continue to email."[9]

4. *Participation by those engaged in diverse disciplines or vocations provides for a more enriching CoLAB experience.* Generally, on a day-to-day basis, people interact with those they know or those working in similar fields or pursuits. This supposition has been confirmed by CoLAB participants who acknowledged that the average number of strangers they speak to about their projects or interests during a given month is three or fewer; this response is pervasive among all age groups and genders. Exceptions are notable: International students studying in the United States have many more conversations with strangers throughout their student careers. Students in journalism and communication fields also have many more conversations with people they don't know, as it is their preference, in general, to talk with people.

   Creativity experts like Todd Siler, author of *Think Like a Genius*, suggest that the most exciting examples of innovative efforts are those that combine two or more drastically different entities, people, places, or things.[10] For instance, what creative idea might emerge when a faculty member in a nursing college becomes involved with a nonprofit museum and a Japanese garden? The answer: a healing program using guided meditation techniques that reduce stress, anxiety, and depression in individuals who regularly visit this type of garden.[11] By combining existing community assets in innovative ways, a new partnership such as this one that realizes a hidden potential can inspire sponsors (such as, in this case, from the Institute of Museum and Library Services) to award grant support to the project. Beyond the benefits of initiating innovative projects and programs, individual participants also derive valuable personal benefits from sharing information about a program, project, or study that is foreign ground to others during the workshop. In postworkshop surveys resulting from two UF CoLABs on Sex and Gender Differences in Health, 76 percent strongly agreed or agreed that as a result of the CoLAB session, "I am more comfortable with people in other disciplines."[12] Additionally, CoLAB organizers have learned that after each successive speed-meeting conversation, many participants consciously work toward honing their message and language. This new ability can have benefits beyond a CoLAB in reducing a participant's isolation from others who don't share a common vocabulary or research expertise.

5. *So much more can be achieved through meetings that encourage multiple conversations.* Consider the case of a typical meeting, workshop, or presentation where one person speaks—someone with authority, who has a unique expertise—while everyone else in the room is silent. Unfortunately, this transfer of information from one person to a large group is highly inefficient when the goal is to share information while building a sense of community within the group. It prohibits any meaningful dialogue with the speaker or conversation among all the others attending who likely have valuable information to share. Think back to the last time you attended a presentation. Did you intentionally sit next to someone you knew? Did you avoid others you did not know? Did you have a meaningful conversation with anyone? These moments can often

feel awkward or uncomfortable. As the presentation progresses one speaker at a time, the entire group listens quietly, shows respect, and occasionally asks a question. You may have sensed that time could have been better spent learning about the people sitting around you. Have you considered that these folks have important information, interests, skills, or resources you might want to learn about?

6. *Having the capacity to appreciate the ambiguousness of a CoLAB Workshop is an important requisite for all participants.* To this end, CoLAB sessions are structured to maximize exposure to large volumes of highly diverse resources— some but not all of which may be of immediate or future benefit to others in the workshop. This makes for a very ambiguous experience. To gain the most benefits when reading others' profiles and engaging in quick conversations, participants must refrain from making snap value judgments about what they read or learn. By suspending their judgment about the quality or applicability of assets that others reveal in their signs and during speed-meetings, participants can move through the speed-meeting rounds with confidence—knowing that the workshop is inherently a valuable experience. CoLABs are intended to expose resources and potential opportunities; the creation of appropriate connections for each participant may occur in an "Aha!" moment at the workshop or it may be triggered later during reflection when participants review others' profile-sign information.

Why Libraries and Library Employees Are Ideal Conveners and Facilitators

Libraries are the ideal location for a CoLAB Workshop, and library staff may be the best people to plan and execute them. CoLABs allow librarians to expand on their already natural roles as conveners and facilitators. Libraries have always connected their patrons to resources and information regardless of format, so why not include people and ideas too? Libraries provide safe, neutral spaces and are often the only institutions that have familiarity with nearly every aspect of their user communities—whether it's a university library that has partnered with numerous academic departments on campus, a public library that has connections with several community organizations in its area, or a K–12 library that has served many of the teachers, administrators, and students in its school. More simply put, libraries have the power to bring together the right people with the right skills and expertise to really benefit one another—the ultimate collaboration matchmakers.

Several libraries already have begun to explore this role with events such as the Human Library (http://humanlibrary.org), a project that originated in Denmark, where attendees can check out living people as "books" who are willing to share their stories with "readers" in an effort to promote human rights and break down stereotypes; or "How-To Festivals" (www.lfpl.org/how-to), where community members gather to teach or share a skill with their fellow neighbors—everything from reading tarot cards to hula hooping to milking a cow. And, of course, there's the makerspace movement where libraries provide the space, tools, and education for users to create, design, and work together in ways they would never be able to do on their own. These kinds of makerspaces can take the form of recording studios, 3-D printing facilities, and sewing stations. Many academic libraries have collaborative spaces in the form of information or scholars commons, outfitted with technology-rich meeting rooms and presentation areas. Others host research symposiums and colloquiums so researchers can share their work with others outside of their disciplines. CoLAB Workshops align perfectly with these kinds of activities and give libraries the opportunity to take their role as information hub one step further.

Collaborating with Strangers events also provide a great opportunity for library staff to communicate who they are, and what they do, to their target audience. While many users are aware of what a library has to offer in terms of space and collections, they may be less familiar with the unique resources and services provided by the actual people who work there. For example, at a Collaborating with Strangers in Education and Communication workshop, an academic librarian explained to a doctoral student that she could connect him with an electronic platform (hosted and supported by the libraries) that would make it possible for his team to publish a new open-access journal. The student previously had no idea the library provided such a service and never would have thought to ask. During CoLABs at UF, numerous Idea Board responses to "What are your next steps?" have been "Follow-up with a librarian!" At a time when the role of librarians and library staff is rapidly evolving, having a venue that continuously serves as an effective outreach tool is incredibly valuable. (See figure 2.11.)

FIGURE 2.11

LIBRARIAN DISCUSSING RESOURCES AND SERVICES WITH A VARIETY OF PARTICIPANTS FROM DIFFERENT DISCIPLINES

Meaningful Outreach

Libraries serve as a much-needed "third space" where patrons can go to learn, connect, recharge, and create—all key components of a CoLAB Workshop. Imagine the total number of possible connections that exist in each of the communities served by libraries—the organizations that could pool resources, the scholars who could combine forces, the neighbors who could learn from one another—and the types of highly focused conversations that could help unlock those connections, conversations that could take place through the CoLAB facilitative process. CoLAB Workshops give libraries the ability to break down silos in the areas they serve, a role that works best in such a trusted, unbiased institution.

NOTES

1. Liz Button, "Steven Johnson Explains 'How We Got to Now,'" American Booksellers Association, Bookselling This Week, February 11, 2015, www.bookweb.org/news/steven-johnson-explains-%E2%80%9Chow-we-got-now%E2%80%9D.

2. Ibid.

3. Steven Johnson, "Where Good Ideas Come From," TED Talk, July 2010, www.ted.com/talks/steven_johnson_where_good_ideas_come_from?language=en.

4. Michael Winer and Karen Ray, *Collaboration Handbook: Creating, Sustaining, and Enjoying the Journey* (Saint Paul, MN: Amherst H. Wilder Foundation, 1996).

5. Bess G. de Farber, *Collaborative Grant-Seeking: A Practical Guide for Librarians* (Lanham, MD: Rowman and Littlefield, 2016), 12–13.

6. John P. Kretzmann and John L. McKnight, *Building Communities from the Inside Out: A Path toward Finding and Mobilizing a Community's Assets* (Evanston, IL: John Kretzmann and John McKnight, 1993).

7. Ibid.

8. Belinda Goldsmith, "Is Surfing the Internet Altering Your Brain?," Reuters, Lifestyle, October 27, 2008, www.reuters.com/article/us-technology-ibrain-idUSTRE49Q34A20081027.

9. Ibid.

10. Todd Siler, *Think Like a Genius* (New York: Bantam Books, 1996).

11. Morikami Museum and Japanese Gardens, "Stroll for Well-Being," accessed October 12, 2015, http://morikami.org/for-adults/stroll-for-well-being.

12. David Miller, "Collaborating with Strangers Workshop for Sex and Gender Differences in Health" (Evaluation report, September 2013), http://ufdc.ufl.edu/IR00008344/00001.

CoLAB Workshop Assessments, Results, and Participant Stories

Learning how to measure the full benefits of a CoLAB Workshop in a tangible way that can be presented to sponsors, stakeholders, and potential participants is essential to the sustainability and growth of future workshops. Once a community, whether a nonprofit, academic, or geographic community, truly understands the value of collaborating with strangers, the possibilities for initiating meaningful connections become endless. Assessing the impact of a CoLAB Workshop involves examining the results of participant experiences and learning as well as the new possibilities for forming partnerships in, or as a follow-up to, the workshop. This can present challenges, however, not commonly found in other types of workshops. Do such facilitative processes really break down barriers and enhance creativity and collaboration? Just how far-reaching is the network of knowledge and ideas that comes from a CoLAB experience?

This chapter presents methods, tools, and strategies for executing various procedures, which involve not only collecting and analyzing the data but also exploring the outcomes gleaned from the workshop data and the experiences of participants.

Preworkshop Surveys

Distributing surveys before the start of a CoLAB Workshop is an effective method for measuring participants' initial feelings about talking to strangers. Preworkshop surveys have asked CoLABers to rate their comfort level with having "face-to-face conversations with others I don't know" and with "talking to 'strangers' with interest, knowledge, and skills different from my own." The preworkshop surveys also have asked participants how often they have conversations with strangers about research, class assignments/projects, career goals/mentoring, and professional passions. Understanding how often attendees interact with those outside their usual circles, and the quality of those conversations, can help the project team better gauge where participants are starting from and how the CoLAB experience may have changed their perspectives.

In a CoLAB that brought together undergraduate public relations students, over 80 percent said they agreed or strongly agreed that they felt comfortable having face-to-face conversations with others they don't know. Yet more than half said they were having fewer than two conversations per month with strangers about class projects and career goals.[1] While this shows that public relations students generally are comfortable talking to people they don't know (not surprising considering their chosen major), they typically are not having the kinds of highly focused conversations—revealing passions and strongest skills—that one often has during a CoLAB Workshop.

Participants also have been asked to share open-ended comments about their experiences talking to strangers in their daily lives. Responses have included positive, negative, and mixed reactions, such as "I feel comfortable talking to strangers in general, but don't really tend to talk about my studies/activities," "I enjoy people and talking/conversing, so I have no anxiety doing so with strangers," "Easier for me in professional settings as opposed to social," and "I am very uncomfortable in groups of strangers but okay with one-on-one interactions."[2]

To implement preworkshop survey activities, CoLAB team members can distribute the survey form (along with a pen, marker, and profile-sign) as participants enter the room. Preworkshop surveys are meant to be brief, usually fitting on a half sheet of paper, and should take fewer than five minutes to complete. Instruct attendees to fill out the survey before the speed-meeting portion of the workshop. Collect the completed surveys or instruct participants to leave them in a designated area before they exit the session. The preworkshop surveys then can be given to either a CoLAB team member in charge of evaluation or a third-party evaluator—usually a paid student assistant, assessment librarian, or researcher specializing in qualitative methods—who will compile results into a detailed evaluation report.

Profile-Signs

Profile-signs themselves can be analyzed to answer questions such as these:

- What disciplines or organizations were represented?
- What kinds of assets and skill sets have been brought together?
- What projects are CoLABers currently working on that could be enhanced by others?

This can be particularly relevant when analyzing topic-based workshops, which often attract a wide variety of participants from diverse backgrounds. In a Collaborating with Strangers on Sustainability Projects at the University of Florida (UF) workshop, forty-six undergraduates, sixteen graduate students, eight faculty, and five staff attended, representing a wide range of academic departments on campus, including accounting, architecture, engineering, sociology, public relations, sculpture, construction management, and the health sciences. Listed skill sets included everything from design techniques and expertise in geographic information system (GIS) software to fundraising, computer programming, and project management. Attendees, who had come to the UF from several cities across the United States and around the world, were involved in ambitious projects such as greenhousing, local gardens, downtown revitalization, and water resource development.[3] Demographic data pulled from profile-signs can tell the stories of rich untapped resources that exist within just one room during a CoLAB Workshop—stories that will resonate well with future sponsors and others (requesters) who may be interested in hosting a workshop in the future.

Observations during a Workshop

CoLAB Workshops are often lively, dynamic experiences that showcase the value of face-to-face conversations. Capturing the data in nonverbal cues (hand gestures, laughter, etc.) as well as the energy and noise levels in the room can be important forms of feedback for the team. How are participants responding to the process? Do they seem inspired and engaged or timid and reserved? A third-party evaluator can serve as an objective witness, jotting down notes and observations about participant interactions (see figure 3.1). In an evaluation report prepared after a series of CoLABs at the University of Florida, David Miller—director of UF's Collaborative Assessment and Program Evaluation Services (CAPES)—summarized these observations:

> Participants often began "speed meetings" hesitantly. However, they quickly saw the value of the meetings. The change in environment was obvious by the third round of "speed meetings." By the third round, there were clearly observable changes with an increase in volume of discussions, participants standing closer together, and greater animation among the participants including pointing at features on each other's signs. Thus, participants were more active in their interactions by the third round.[4]

FIGURE 3.1

EXTERNAL EVALUATOR RECORDING OBSERVATIONS DURING A CoLAB

Photo by
Barbara Hood

In one CoLAB, a participant was heard to say, "If I knew it was going to be like this I never would have come!" As an introvert, she initially wasn't comfortable with the idea of having so many one-on-one conversations with strangers but appeared more relaxed and animated with each round. By the end of the session, she was enthusiastically adding her responses to the Idea Boards and had identified several synergies and next steps. Other pairs have been observed giving each other a high-five and one participant yelled out, "You're just like me!" at a CoLAB titled Books and Objects of Study. These observations can be helpful contributions to the evaluation process. The team should be sure to position the observing evaluator in an area where he or she can easily pick up on interactions but still appear inconspicuous to participants. Observations can be recorded on a notepad, laptop, or iPad and summarized in a report for the CoLAB team. Recording observations, especially through an outside perspective, allows the team to access data they may have otherwise missed.

Idea Boards

At some point during a CoLAB Workshop, often as the final activity, attendees are asked to briefly jot down on Post-it notes the answers to three questions and affix them on "Idea Boards" situated around the room (see chapter 4 for details about this process):

1. What synergies (or connections) did you discover?
2. What did you learn?
3. What are your next steps?

The responses to these questions capture information about initial connections, discoveries, and goals while they are still fresh in the minds of participants and can be especially telling for evaluation purposes. For example, in a CoLAB bringing together graduate student associations in education and in communications, it was easy to visualize exactly where the two disciplines intersected. Answers to "What synergies did you discover?" included responses such as "interest in social divides," "open educational resources," "big data," and "So many of us are interested in social media analysis!"[5] Synergies discovered while analyzing the Idea Board responses in another CoLAB Workshop, titled Sex and Gender Differences in Health, revealed participants' common interests in health literacy, health care access disparities, and research on attitudes toward exercise. Often, connections revealed on the Idea Board for the first question go far beyond the expectations of participants (and the CoLAB team) and provide valuable insights into collaborative opportunities for attendees (see figure 3.2).

The CoLAB team also can evaluate the kinds of "matches" made at a workshop from the responses to the synergies question. In a CoLAB presented to a grant-writing class (open to all majors), two students quickly discovered that they both were researching elephants, but from completely different disciplinary lenses. While their approaches and methodology were different, each student's experiences certainly had the potential to inform the other's work. Even though these students were taking the same grant-writing class, they most likely would not have made this discovery on their own if it were not for the CoLAB process.

FIGURE 3.2

SYNERGIES POSTED ON IDEA BOARD DURING MASS COMMUNICATIONS AND HEALTH CoLAB

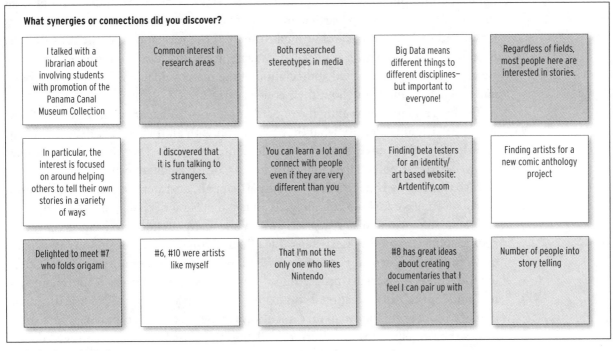

What synergies or connections did you discover?

I talked with a librarian about involving students with promotion of the Panama Canal Museum Collection	Common interest in research areas	Both researched stereotypes in media	Big Data means different things to different disciplines—but important to everyone!	Regardless of fields, most people here are interested in stories.
In particular, the interest is focused on around helping others to tell their own stories in a variety of ways	I discovered that it is fun talking to strangers.	You can learn a lot and connect with people even if they are very different than you	Finding beta testers for an identity/ art based website: Artdentify.com	Finding artists for a new comic anthology project
Delighted to meet #7 who folds origami	#6, #10 were artists like myself	That I'm not the only one who likes Nintendo	#8 has great ideas about creating documentaries that I feel I can pair up with	Number of people into story telling

Photo by Bess de Farber

Asking participants what they learned also is a great way to determine the breadth of ideas, information, and resources exchanged during a CoLAB Workshop. Even if participants never pursue collaborative relationships with their fellow CoLABers after the workshop, the acquisition of new knowledge alone has been a consistent outcome of immeasurable value for participants. For example, at a CoLAB Workshop bringing together subject librarians from different branches on campus, attendees stated they learned everything from "Empathy is a skill in organizational leadership" to "There are varying definitions of statistics and data management" to "French decadence is a field of study."[6] One participant even said she learned which of her research projects seemed to attract the most interest from her peers, while another came away with a list of contacts for questions and information about a variety of topics she was interested in. During a similar CoLAB at the University of North Texas, librarians discovered that a common interest among almost all participants was social justice issues.

Many participants will respond to the "What did you learn?" question with answers that reflect just how affected they were by the CoLAB experience. For example, representatives of nonprofit organizations at the HIV/AIDS Prevention in Youth CoLAB learned "the power of connection to others," "different ways to analyze assets of an agency," and "Even though our organizations have different titles, we all have similar goals."[7]

Also, when participants share what they've learned, the CoLAB team can easily assess what the key takeaways of the session were. In a CoLAB attended by students, faculty, and librarians, the team was pleasantly surprised to see librarians and library-related content mentioned several times on the Idea Boards. Student comments included these:

"Librarians can give lots of ideas about resources on all topics," "Librarians connect people with information," and "Google Scholar is not as good as Web of Science."[8] Other than in the context of highly focused environments such as those found at CoLABs, librarians don't often get the opportunity to talk one-on-one with students about what they do. At this workshop, participants undeniably were affected by the conversations they'd had with librarians and wanted to share those revelations on the Idea Boards. Even if these participants, especially students, took little else from the session, they clearly expressed an elevated appreciation of the many valuable ways in which librarians can help them throughout their college careers.

The final and most revealing Idea Board question—"What are your next steps?"—is where participants identify what they plan to do with all the new connections, ideas, knowledge, and resources they have acquired throughout the workshop. This is another way to determine potential ongoing impacts of CoLAB facilitative processes. In various CoLABs held at the University of Florida, participants' next steps included "Follow up at a local meeting we are both attending," "Contact that Senior Scholar, introduce myself!," and "Send info on oral histories program."[9] While many attendees will explain how they plan to follow up on the "next steps" Idea Board, others will describe ways to expand on what they've learned. For example, "Follow leads for a literature review," "Check out the AEJMC conference proceedings," "Find a new book that was recommended to me," and "Specify an educational context for my dissertation topic."[10] While the intention of CoLABers to follow up may not always come to fruition, capturing "next steps" allows the workshop team to learn of collaborative possibilities that emerged during the workshop—as seen through the eyes of participants.

When gathering Idea Board responses for evaluation purposes, it is important to label each Post-it with its corresponding question number before removing it from the board. You also can take a photo of each board to capture all of the responses, but be sure to verify that responses are legible if the team plans to rely on the photograph for this content. Transcribe the answers under each question in a Word document and submit it to either a member of the team or a third-party evaluator. Be sure to transcribe comments exactly; if a participant writes a word in all capital letters with three exclamation marks next to it, include that too. The person responsible for evaluating the Idea Board comments can then code the responses into like categories in an effort to identify trends, for example: How many attendees referenced a connection with a particular person? What kinds of knowledge and new resources did participants describe? How many listed specific plans to follow up? Idea Board responses can help to answer these questions easily while offering valuable insights to the project team.

Idea Tables

During a CoLAB Workshop presented for organizations, Idea Tables can serve as a more group-oriented alternative to Idea Boards. At Idea Tables, organization representatives have been encouraged to review their checklist notes and individually brainstorm a list of future partnership ideas based on the many conversations they had during the speed-meeting process. They then share potential partnership ideas with other representatives at their table (see figure 3.3). This debriefing can be expected to generate even more ideas. Finally, all lists are collected and transcribed by the team into a PowerPoint presentation (between workshop sessions if a series is planned) that is shared with all attendees, further perpetuating ideas among the larger group. Not only does this give participants an opportunity to reflect and plan next steps, but the list of partnership ideas also offers key insights about the potential impact of CoLAB Workshops. When barriers are eliminated and organization representatives serving the same geographic area are brought together in a meaningful way, what kinds of new, innovative collaborations arise? Activities that occur at Idea Tables can answer this question.

At a Palm Beach County CoLAB, for example, the Alzheimer's Community Care organization representative listed several possible project ideas to partner with other nonprofits in the local area, such as providing access to food from a local food bank for eligible patients, a support group and education luncheon with the Glades Health Care Center, a joint grant to address racially biased medical care discrepancies with TMPU (Toward a More Perfect Union), and representation at a Palm Beach College health fair to inform on Alzheimer's disease. The Glades Area Boys and Girls Club listed one-on-one tutors from the Literacy Coalition, teen training with the Anti-Defamation League, and a youth arts program with the Armory Arts Center among many other potential projects with new partners. Such partnership ideas showcase the wide variety

FIGURE 3.3

PARTICIPANTS AT AN IDEA TABLE FOR A REGIONAL NONPROFIT ORGANIZATION CoLAB IN BOCA RATON, FLORIDA

Photo from the Junior League Boca Raton newsletter

of powerful connections that can arise from a CoLAB and give the evaluation team the opportunity to track those partnerships and their development over time.

Postworkshop Surveys

Adding a brief postworkshop survey to the back of the profile-signs to be filled out immediately following the session is an effective method for gaining understanding about how participants viewed their overall CoLAB experience and its value (see figure 3.4). At the UF CoLABs, surveys have included questions such as these:

- Would you attend a workshop like this again?
- Would you recommend the CoLAB process to other students and faculty?
- Has this experience helped you realize the value of speaking to people you do not know about their passions and assets?

A Likert scale is used to allow participants to rate how much they agree or disagree with such statements as "I feel more comfortable in my ability to approach people I don't know" and "I feel more comfortable talking to strangers in different disciplines" as an immediate response to the CoLAB experience. The postworkshop survey concludes with a series of open-ended questions that ask attendees to describe any new knowledge or resources they acquired, the most useful part of the workshop, and what surprised them about the speed-meeting process.

In a comprehensive evaluation report compiled after a series of CoLAB Workshops at UF, postworkshop survey findings revealed that 93 percent of participants rated the workshop good or excellent. When asked if they would attend a workshop like this again, 88 percent responded positively and 90 percent said they would recommend the workshop to other students and faculty. Even more significant to the workshop team was that 77 percent of participants reported that they "felt more confident approaching people they do not know" after their CoLAB experience.[11]

While these results overwhelmingly show that participants are walking away with a positive CoLAB experience, it's the open-ended comments that essentially highlight which elements made a lasting impression. For example, when asked in the postworkshop survey, "Did the CoLAB facilitation process help you access new resources or knowledge?" attendees provided answers such as these: "The ideas from the non-related disciplines were very helpful. It was like 'out of box' thinking"; "Yes, I met people dealing with homeless people and animals. I've learned a lot from them. I like this"; "Yes, I spoke to a grant writer, learned about internship opportunities and the health disparity minor"; "Yes, it helped me meet many people I would have never met and talk to people doing research pertaining to gender and sex."[12]

Learning what participants feel was the most useful part of the workshop helps the team determine which workshop activities are having the largest impact on CoLABers. Answers to this question often include responses like these: "Probably learning to convey my research and interests to others quickly, effectively"; "Helping me approach people better because it's something I need to work on"; "Feeling more comfortable talking to people of higher academic ranks"; "Hearing different perspectives on the same issues."[13] Participants repeatedly mention their conversations with strangers, and the resources and knowledge gained from those conversations, as the most beneficial part of a CoLAB Workshop.

In some sessions, participants have been asked what part of the CoLAB presentation they found most useful. This question allows the team to determine which of the CoLAB principles or concepts resonated most with attendees. For example, in one CoLAB Workshop, some participants reported learning the difference between collaboration, cooperation, and coordination as the most useful part; others appreciated the tips on enhancing creativity; and several more were interested in the concept of "asset based community development." Participants often have described feeling inspired by the video clip from Steven Johnson's TED Talk "Where Good Ideas Come From" as well as the African proverb that starts every CoLAB presentation: "If you want to go fast, go alone. If you want to go far, go together."

FIGURE 3.4

POSTWORKSHOP SURVEY

(Complete at the end of the session.)

1. My overall CoLAB evaluation: ___ Excellent ___ Good ___ Fair ___ Poor

2. I would attend a workshop like this again: ___ Yes ___ No

3. I would recommend this collaboration process to other students/faculty: ___ Yes ___ No

4. Has this experience helped you realize the value of speaking to people you do not know about their assets, skills, and passions? ___ Yes ___ No

5. CoLAB Results: ___ Strongly Agree ___ Agree ___ Neutral ___ Disagree ___ Strongly Disagree
   - ☐ I feel more confident in my ability to approach people I don't know.
   - ☐ I am more comfortable talking to "strangers" in different disciplines.
   - ☐ (If applicable) I am more comfortable talking to "strangers" in different positions in their academic or professional careers (e.g., student to faculty).

6. Did the CoLAB facilitation process help you access new resources, knowledge, and/or grant-seeking information? If so, please describe:

   _____

   _____

7. What was the most useful part of the workshop and why?

   _____

   _____

8. What surprised you about the speed-meeting process?

   _____

   _____

9. During the presentation, what information was most useful and/or interesting?

   _____

   _____

10. Would you be willing to participate in a twenty-minute follow-up interview in the next two to three months?
    ___ Yes ___ No   Please list e-mail if Yes: _____

Asking attendees what surprised them most about the speed-meeting process usually reveals the remarkable difference between participants' expectations as they arrive at a CoLAB Workshop and their actual experience. In a Collaborating with Strangers on Internationalization workshop, participants said they were surprised by "how quickly 3 minutes goes by," "how easy it would be and how much I learned about others," "how engaged people were," and "how often we were looking to solve similar challenges."[14] The fact that CoLABers are usually surprised by how fun, painless, and beneficial talking to strangers can be shows just how much anxiety, or fear of the unknown, can serve as a major barrier to face-to-face collaboration.

Postworkshop surveys also are a powerful tool for evaluating CoLAB Workshops that bring together nonprofit organizations (see figure 3.5). The questions can be slightly modified to assess whether the CoLAB process is truly effective in meeting the collaborative goals of organizations. For example, in a CoLAB Workshop with nonprofits in Palm Beach County, Florida, representatives from each group answered questions about their overall experience. Comments included these: "The encouragement to mix and mingle, but in a structured way, was very positive and helped open doors that would otherwise remain shut or unseen"; "We have a greater awareness of nonprofit organizations in our area, particularly in the social service sector, and a greater sense of how dissimilar organizations can share resources to serve a variety of populations"; "I realized that we weren't quite ready for collaborations at this point in time . . . but it was a great way to explore our reasons to connect with Belle Glade further;" "The process of connection and discovery creates an environment in which many services can be improved or invented. Even those not yet imagined."[15]

Postworkshop surveys work best when printed on the back of profile-signs, as this cuts back on extra paper and reduces the chance of lost surveys. Similar to preworkshop surveys, the signs are distributed by the CoLAB team as participants first enter the room. CoLABers are encouraged to complete the surveys at the end of the workshop (in pen, not marker), and to be as thorough as possible in the comment sections. Having a team member stationed at the door to collect profile-signs as participants leave (sometimes before the session is over) and to remind them to complete the survey, if they haven't already, ensures a larger number of signs will be analyzed for more accurate assessment results. Once all profile-signs have been collected, a team member can scan the surveys and send them to an evaluation team member or third-party evaluator. Results should be compiled into a detailed evaluation report for the CoLAB team, sponsor(s), or workshop requester.

Follow-Up Interviews

After a CoLAB Workshop has ended, the team will wonder who actually followed up, what kinds of connections were made, and what the ultimate results of those connections were. How many partnerships, projects, and innovative ideas can be traced back to a CoLAB experience? The best way to answer this question is to conduct interviews with past participants, preferably at least two months after the initial workshop. For example, when one student who participated in a Sex and Gender Differences in Health

FIGURE 3.5

POSTWORKSHOP SURVEY FOR NONPROFIT ORGANIZATIONS

1. Did the workshop meet, exceed, or not meet your expectations? (Circle answer.)
   Comments:

   _____

   _____

   _____

2. Were there components of the workshop that will be immediately applicable to operations within your organization(s)?
   If yes, please list three applicable components:

   _____

   _____

   _____

Please rank the presentation: circle the appropriate number (5 is highest quality):

Overall quality of presentation	5	4	3	2	1
Effective use of time during the presentation	5	4	3	2	1
Interaction/participation by attendees	5	4	3	2	1
Usefulness of information	5	4	3	2	1

Comments:

_____

_____

What did you get out of the speed-meeting process?

_____

_____

In what ways were the Idea Tables beneficial or not?

_____

_____

How will the book of profile-signs be beneficial or not?

_____

_____

Based on the quality of this workshop, would you consider participating in future CoLAB Workshops or recommending that others attend these workshops?

_____

_____

CoLAB was asked in an interview if she had followed up with anyone she met at the workshop, she responded:

> I did follow up with another participant. He's in a different stage of his career than I am, but he actually just e-mailed me yesterday with a job opportunity within his lab and it's a really good job. And he offered to help me in any way he could, he's a grad student and I'm an undergrad. It was great timing, he just emailed me yesterday, but we did meet for coffee before that too.[16]

Another CoLAB participant, an associate dean for research in the College of Journalism and Communications, described a Collaborating with Strangers in Communications and Health event as an amazing experience that sparked several collaborations between faculty and researchers from both colleges:

> There were follow-ups with the College of Public Health and Health Professions. We did set up face-to-face meetings with some of them as a result of the CoLAB. We ended up forming a co-master's degree where students in the College of Public Health can take a series of our classes as an option. So yes, that definitely, that's what came of it.[17]

One-on-one interviews also are an effective method for discovering unexpected connections or benefits from a CoLAB experience. One graduate student explained in a follow-up interview that participating in a CoLAB during her grant-writing class actually helped her to decide between multiple dissertation topics, as well as how to best explain her research to those outside of her discipline:

> I researched several things so when actually having to do the CoLAB and having to then explain it to someone else, I found myself explaining one specific leg of my research, which then also helped me see that this is the leg that's most palatable to everyone, you know what I mean? So that helped me select it for my dissertation. So part of it, due to the CoLAB, helped me to realize that you have to talk about your research for people to realize that they might want to include you in grants or that they might want to include you in publications. The CoLAB experience for me was more about starting to think how I can explain to people my usefulness.[18]

A common theme often revealed in follow-up interviews is the role CoLAB Workshops can play in connecting participants to new resources, knowledge, and ideas. As one interviewee explained:

> I really liked the activity because even if you do not actually talk to others after the event, I think it has a big impact because it definitely opens your mind to different paths other people take and honestly going there as an undergraduate I really loved it. I feel sometimes we're actually kind of segregated, like not intentionally but there's just not that exchange of knowledge every day. So it helped me to see that there's definitely research out there and people that

would definitely participate with you on your projects and that pretty much you're not alone.[19]

One faculty member even described learning of a possible funding source from another CoLAB participant that could help extend the visibility of her research:

> I found out that there's a fund where there might be money available to pay for publication in an open access journal. In the particular topic for which I'm doing this grant proposal there is an open access journal that is very highly cited but it's like $1,500 to publish in and I would not otherwise do that.[20]

She also expressed excitement at being connected to a resource person who could fulfill a need in her work:

> I was really looking for a statistician but didn't really have a clue how, you know, we don't have any real statistician-type people in-house. I didn't really have a sense of, well gosh, where would I find that person? And now I do. One of the people I met at the CoLAB, that's what he does. So next time I need a statistician I probably will be going back to that person and contacting him about either coming on board or recommending somebody else.[21]

Understanding how the CoLAB Workshop efficiently breaks down barriers and connects those who would never ordinarily cross paths is another benefit to conducting follow-up interviews with past participants. Said one graduate student:

> I would say the main benefit of the CoLAB for me was having all those people in one place because just scheduling and committing to two hours, or thirty minutes, or a five minute conversation is a big deal for many people so that was really helpful. If I needed to reach out to one of the people who participated it would be so much easier now that you had the first networking step, to say, hey, we were in the same CoLAB and now I'm thinking of this project.[22]

When planning to conduct follow-up interviews with past participants, it is best to include a question in the postworkshop survey asking attendees whether they would be willing to participate in a twenty-minute follow-up interview. Collect contact information (names, e-mail addresses, department, etc.) from those who answer "yes" and enter data into a shared spreadsheet. The interviewer then can contact willing participants via e-mail to schedule in-person, telephone, or video chat meetings. Keep track of those who have been contacted, their responses, and whether or not they have been interviewed. A member of the workshop team can conduct the interviews, but ideally, a third-party evaluator can provide a sense of objectivity that will yield the best data. Interviews should be recorded using a high-quality digital recorder and transcribed for later analysis. Upload text and audio files to a cloud-based folder, such as Dropbox, and give all team members access. Interviewees can be asked questions such as these: "In what ways was your experience at the CoLAB a success?" "In what ways did you feel limited in your CoLAB experience?" "Did you use the CoLAB webpage to continue networking with fellow participants? If so . . ." "Do you feel more connected to resources and important assets?" (See also the sidebar.)

SAMPLE INTERVIEW QUESTIONS FOR PREVIOUS CoLAB WORKSHOP PARTICIPANTS

1. Did you feel comfortable talking with your partners?
2. Did the format of the workshop impact your comfort? (Three-minute "speed-meetings," participant profile-signs, etc.)
3. In what ways was your experience at the CoLAB a success?
4. What did you learn? What did you gain?
5. Did you feel like you were set up for success at the workshop? Why or why not? In what ways?
6. In what ways did you feel limited in your CoLAB experience?
7. How were your relationships with your partners? How did the format impact your overall experience?
8. Did you use the online follow-up to continue networking with fellow participants? Why or why not? In what ways?
9. Do you think you were able to improve your networking skills? With people in other fields, disciplines, and positions?
10. Do you feel more connected to resources and important assets in your community? In what ways?
11. What are different resources that you feel you can tap into after your CoLAB experience? (New people, new departments, new facilities/organizations, etc.)
12. How do you feel about collaborating with other people? Personally? In research? In team projects?
13. Did your view on collaborative relationships change as a result of your CoLAB experience?
14. Are you more or less likely to engage in collaborative relationships after your workshop experience?
15. Were you able to generate new ideas for research?
16. How did being introduced to researchers outside of your field/discipline impact your ideas?
17. What was the most important thing you learned at the CoLAB Workshop? About others? About yourself?

Anecdotal Stories

There often will be times when a past participant will approach or contact a member of the team with an anecdote about his or her CoLAB experience. For example, one CoLABer recognized a team member while waiting in line at a sandwich shop and began excitedly sharing her story. As a graduate student, she had attended a Collaborating with Strangers for Grant Seeking workshop and met another participant who helped her create an image-only tutorial to teach farmers in Guatemala how to use new farming technology. The problem with delivering training programs in Guatemala, she shared, is that so many different dialects are spoken there, which creates a language barrier that's difficult to break. She was extremely grateful to have found a partner to help complete such an important project.

Another team member spoke to a sustainable buildings coordinator at UF who said he considered himself a "CoLAB junkie"; he had been to several Collaborating with Strangers workshops around campus and was already working on three separate projects with collaborators he had met earlier that year. And yet another heard from a colleague that an evolutionary biologist, seeking to make science more accessible to the general public, had initiated a campus-wide insect-inspired art exhibit that involved many university partners, including the science library. According to the biologist, it was at a CoLAB Workshop that she initially realized she could plan exhibits with the libraries, which evolved into working with the Harn Museum of Art and the UF Department of Forestry.

While some attendees will share their experiences months or even years after a CoLAB workshop has ended, others will approach the team immediately following a session with such comments as "I have to admit I was nervous in the beginning, but by the end I had forgotten all about it" or "I found so many potential guest speakers for my class!" Participants also will recommend topics for future sessions—"We should do one of these on open access" or "It would be great if we could do a CoLAB with the College of Business"—as well as comments on what they found most useful or interesting—"I loved this. Really humanizes the people in our cohort."[23]

In addition to participants' sharing anecdotes during run-ins with team members, many requesters will follow up with e-mails or letters summarizing their feedback on the CoLAB Workshop experience. After a session was conducted for a class of doctoral students in the College of Journalism and Communications, the instructor sent a thank-you e-mail to team members with the subject line "WOW!!!" and this message: "Feedback has been amazing!!!! Can I go ahead and schedule you for next semester for the same class?? This was wonderful—they LOVED it!"[24] Another faculty member, and director of UF's Center for the Humanities and the Public Sphere, wrote, "The 'social capital' that we created at this event is continuing to bear fruit, in the form of grant proposals, faculty working groups, and team taught courses," in a letter of support for a CoLAB Workshops grant proposal.[25]

After a CoLAB for faculty in UF's College of the Arts, the dean emeritus who had requested the session followed up with a letter that stated:

The response from the 100+ faculty in attendance was uniformly positive. Many of them talked together for the first time and learned about similar interests. I was particularly pleased that several faculty became involved in ongoing projects as a result of their CoLAB experience. In summary, CoLAB accomplished more in one hour than we had been able to achieve in 15 years.[26]

On occasion, a past CoLAB participant will be so enthusiastic about sharing his or her story that he or she is willing to write a short narrative that can be submitted to the team and added to evaluation materials. For example, one graduate student in the English department reflected on her CoLAB experience at a Collaborating with Strangers on Books and Objects of Study workshop:

The three-minute time limit demanded that the participants articulate their interests succinctly and quickly find patterns or minute commonalities. This is a beneficial exercise for young scholars to practice. The fellow participants with similar interests but different expertise gave great feedback on budding ideas, and I walked away with a new understanding of the resources available on campus.[27]

Another past participant, this time an adult programs and volunteer coordinator at an art museum, wrote the following in her narrative:

I surprisingly had something to offer everyone I met—whether a good laugh, advice about navigating the university or a different perspective on a social issue with research implications. I left feeling empowered, more knowledgeable and happy. The conversations I had were great, especially because the clock was ticking. Time felt very valuable.[28]

What exactly can anecdotal data offer the CoLAB team, and how can it be collected and disseminated in a concrete way? Capturing the informal comments and stories of past participants allows the team to further answer this burning question: *What happens after someone leaves a CoLAB Workshop?* What connections were established and how have those partnerships continued to evolve and grow? What were the immediate benefits, and what can be done to improve CoLAB Workshops in the future? The eagerness with which participants are willing to share such information is telling in itself, and the CoLAB team should give as much attention and credit to this kind of data as they do to any other evaluation method.

The long-term effects of CoLAB Workshops are difficult to track beyond one-on-one interviews. Anecdotal data can bring the team interesting and useful information they would otherwise miss. When approached with participant comments or stories, either in person or via e-mail, team members should immediately jot down or copy the information as completely as possible. Transfer quotes, comments, or narratives into a spreadsheet with as much demographic information as possible. Recording and collecting anecdotal data in one place will allow the team to reference participant quotes and stories easily and efficiently. Participant testimonials and first-person accounts are essential for making a "Why does this matter?" case to funders and stakeholders.

While assessing CoLAB Workshops can be challenging and time-consuming, the methods discussed here are effective for accessing and analyzing data to evaluate the ongoing impact of collaborating with strangers. Whether it is understanding participant comfort levels with face-to-face conversations, learning how attendees viewed their overall experience, or discovering the types of knowledge, skills, resources, and collaborative partnerships that originate from such workshops, each method offers unique data that further illustrates the substantial value of CoLAB facilitative processes. Sponsors, workshop requesters, and potential participants are going to ask the essential questions: "Does this really work?" and "What's in it for me?" The ability to demonstrate, through proven evaluation methods, how CoLAB Workshops break down barriers and create a culture of collaboration and innovation among any community is worth the requisite time and effort.

NOTES

1. David Miller, "Collaborating with Strangers Workshop Evaluation Reports: Feb 2014 Internationalization CoLAB Evaluation Report" (PDF document, 2014), http://ufdc.ufl.edu/IR00008344/00001.

2. Ibid.

3. David Miller, "Collaborating with Strangers Workshop Evaluation Reports: feb2013 CoLAB on Sustainability Evaluation Report" (PDF document, 2013), http://ufdc.ufl.edu/IR00008344/00001.

4. David Miller, "Collaborating with Strangers Workshop Evaluation Reports: comp12–13" (PDF document, 2013), http://ufdc.ufl.edu/IR00008344/00001.

5. April Hines, "Collaborating with Strangers in Education and Communication Idea Board Comments" (PDF document, 2016), http://ufdc.ufl.edu//IR00008482/00001.

6. April Hines, "Collaborating with Strangers on Research and Scholarship Idea Board Comments" (PDF document, 2016), http://ufdc.ufl.edu//IR00008481/00001.

7. Bess de Farber, "HIV/Aids Prevention in Youth CoLAB Evaluation Report" (Word document, 2003), http://ufdc.ufl.edu//IR00008478/00001.

8. April Hines, "Selected Quotes from Various CoLAB Workshop Participant Feedback: 2002 through 2014" (Word document, 2016), http://ufdc.ufl.edu/IR00008471/00001, 1.

9. Ibid.

10. Ibid.

11. Miller, "Workshop Evaluation Reports: comp12-13."

12. Hines, "Selected Quotes," 2.

13. Ibid.

14. Miller, "Workshop Evaluation Reports: Feb 2014."

15. Hines, "Selected Quotes," 3.

16. CoLAB participant, interview by Alexandrea Matthews, May 8, 2014, interview 2, transcript.

17. CoLAB participant, interview by Alexandrea Matthews, March 20, 2015, interview 14, transcript.

18. CoLAB participant, interview by Alexandrea Matthews, March 25, 2015, interview 15, transcript.

19. CoLAB participant, interview by Alexandrea Matthews, September 26, 2014, interview 10, transcript.

20. CoLAB participant, interview by Alexandrea Matthews, May 15, 2014, interview 5, transcript.

21. Ibid.

22. CoLAB participant, interview by Alexandrea Matthews, May 9, 2014, interview 3, transcript.

23. April Hines, "Anecdotal Comments from Participants after CoLAB Workshops at the University of Florida (2009–2016)" (Word document, 2016), http://ufdc.ufl.edu//IR00008479/00001, 2.

24. Ibid.

25. April Hines, "Mini Grant: 'Collaborating with Strangers In and Outside Mass Communications': Mini Grant Application Packet" (PDF document, October 2013), http://ufdc.ufl.edu/IR00003574/00001, 14.

26. Hines, "Anecdotal Comments," 2.

27. Hines, "Mini Grant," 12.

28. Emily Brooks, "Narrative Reflections after Collaborating with Strangers on Books and Objects of Study Workshop" (Word document, 2016), http://ufdc.ufl.edu//IR00008480/00001.

Step-by-Step Instructions for Conducting CoLAB Workshops

4

To describe and simulate all of the steps related to presenting your first CoLAB Workshop, this chapter illustrates four sample scenarios for workshops taking place in (1) an on-campus environment (gallery space, conference or training room, lecture hall), (2) an academic library, (3) a classroom as part of a course, and (4) a community location (public library, community foundation, United Way, or other training or convening facility).

Some of the steps described here will be identical for all types of collaboration workshops, and others will be unique to only one particular workshop type. Each workshop scenario details the Collaborating with Strangers model that features an agenda between two and three and one-half hours in length. All of the steps presented are based on best practices developed since the first CoLAB Workshop was held in 2002.

Scenario 1: On-Campus Space (Not in a Library) CoLAB Workshop

To describe this first scenario, let's say that the journalism librarian has received a request from a communications faculty member to facilitate a collaboration (CoLAB) workshop for students and faculty working in journalism and communication studies. Participants who choose to attend will be eligible to apply for mini-grant funding to support a collaborative research project. The faculty member explains that the purpose of the workshop is to help faculty and students (1) identify those potential project participants who may have similar interests, (2) find those who have access to a variety of assets, and (3) spark ideas for projects that are innovative while leveraging assets that are readily available. The communications professor seeks to inspire teams to submit project proposals for available funding of up to $1,500 per project.

A QUICK TIP

When meeting with the requester, be sure to emphasize that CoLAB Workshops, while driven by guiding principles, can be customized to meet the unique needs of the participants. Profile-signs may be color coded to identify participants from varying groups, and questions can be modified to coincide with the desired outcomes of the workshop. For example, in a previous Internationalization CoLAB, students were asked what kinds of international programs, classes, or events they had participated in during their college career and how those experiences had enhanced their multicultural understanding.

Preworkshop Activities for Scenario 1

Step 1: Create a CoLAB team and meet with the communications professor.

The CoLAB team usually consists of those library employees who have expertise in facilitation, instruction, promotion, and coordination of library events. In this case, the team should include, at the very least, the journalism and communications librarian and another colleague with this expertise. Schedule a meeting to plan the workshop with the requesting faculty member and follow the agenda in table 4.1.

Step 2: Prepare the design of the electronic and print postcard and the poster.

The CoLAB team designs the workshop promotional materials and decides on the title, Collaborating with Strangers for Mini-grant Communications Projects. The image selected to brand the workshop was chosen from copyright-free images found on the Web by searching for "communications images" and "communications project images."

MODIFIED STANDARD TEXT USED FOR ACADEMIC SETTINGS FOR THE POSTCARD AND POSTER

Hey, Stranger . . . Looking for a way to apply for funding for your collaborative communications research or service project? Collaborating with Strangers workshops connect students and faculty on campus during three-minute speed-meetings. You could walk away with great ideas, access to new resources, and meet talented people who would be interested in joining you to apply for a $1,500 collaboration Mini-grant award.

When: Wednesday, October 1, 2:30 to 4:30 p.m.
Where: College of Journalism and Communications (CJC), conference room 100
Who: Any faculty or students in Journalism and Communications Studies who are working on research or service projects

Information and registration: <link>
Refreshments will be served.

An e-mail message is sent to the communications professor along with the draft electronic versions of the postcard and poster. The professor responds with a list of workshop sponsors to add to the promotional materials, including the Communications Student Association. Revisions are made, sent, and approved by the professor.

TABLE 4.1

AGENDA FOR AN HOUR PLANNING MEETING WITH THE COMMUNICATIONS PROFESSOR

TIME	ACTIVITY
10 minutes	Give an overview of a typical CoLAB Workshop, its purpose of connecting strangers with one another's assets, its possible length, and options for workshop agenda activities.
10 minutes	Learn more about the communications professor's desired outcomes to determine if these are feasible for the length of time available during the workshop. (Everyone agrees that the workshop will be two hours long. This means that at least twelve students and faculty will meet one another: 12 conversations × 4 minutes = 48 minutes + 45 minutes for preparing profile-signs and completing the PowerPoint presentation + plus another 20 minutes to complete Idea Boards and evaluations.)
35 minutes	Once the length of the workshop has been decided, then through a consensus-building conversation led by the facilitators, develop answers to the following questions: • Other than the facilitators, who else will present at the workshop? (Answer: The communications professor will provide brief opening remarks, including introduction of the CoLAB team, description of the mini-grant funding opportunity and guidelines, acknowledgment of sponsors and staff who contributed to the workshop promotion and preparation, and enthusiasm for the potential connections that will be discovered. This will take no more than five minutes.) • How many participants are anticipated and what is the minimum number of participants to conduct the workshop? (Answer: For this scenario, a total of twenty-four participants is anticipated; a minimum of fourteen participants is required to hold the workshop.) • What is the optimal participant ratio of faculty to students? (Answer: 1:1.) • How many conversations is the workshop team anticipating that the agenda will accommodate? (The typical number of speed-meeting rounds will be between twelve and seventeen during a workshop that lasts two to two and one-half hours. To determine the anticipated number of rounds, divide the amount of time devoted to the speed-meeting activity by four minutes. So one hour will yield the possibility of twelve to fifteen conversations.) • What questions will be used on the profile-sign? (Answer: The facilitators have suggested questions for the profile-signs, and during the discussion, the team has agreed to use these questions: (1) What is your current research or service project interest and why are you passionate about this work? (2) What recent collaborative projects have you been involved in, and what was your role? (3) What are your skills and strengths? (4) What networks, associations, or other groups do you participate in? (5) What is one thing most people don't know about you?) • Where will the workshop be presented? (Answer: This workshop will take place in a conference room, which features round tables with four chairs at each table, at the College of Journalism and Communications. The room contains a computer, screen, and projector. There is plenty of walking space to accommodate thirty participants as they move from one conversation to another. No room setup is required. The team agrees to visit the conference room prior to the workshop date to plan for how the space will be used during the workshop.) • What date and time will the workshop be presented? (Answer: October 1 from 2:00 to 4:00 p.m.) • Who will lead the efforts to promote the workshop and provide information about registration? (Answer: The event coordinator in the College of Journalism and Communications will send the e-mail promotion(s), print and distribute postcards, and hang posters. The CoLAB team will design the electronic and print postcards and the poster.) • When will promotion of the workshop begin? (Answer: Four weeks prior to the workshop date, on September 1.) • Who will manage the registration process and the correspondence with registered participants? (Answer: The College of Journalism and Communications events coordinator will set up the registration electronic link to coincide with the promotion kickoff and will correspond with registrants. The CoLAB team will provide a template for the workshop confirmation e-mail message and for the reminder e-mail message.) • How will the workshop be evaluated and by whom? (Answer: A librarian with assessment expertise will design the evaluation plan and instrument, and will maintain a neutral observation role during the workshop.) • Who will provide refreshments? (Answer: The College of Journalism and Communications will provide bottled water and cookies.)
5 minutes	• Review all the confirmed decisions and follow-up actions, along with persons responsible for each action, to reduce confusion and misunderstandings.

After providing the promotional e-poster and the e-mail message, ask the requester to push out this content through CJC's internal channels—social media, e-mail discussion lists, flyers in designated spaces, classroom announcements, and so forth. Participants are more likely to show interest in an event that has been endorsed by a dean, professor, college, or organization rather than one merely promoted by the library.

Step 3: Prepare a workshop promotion plan and share it with the promoters at the CJC.

This will provide a list of ideas for promoting the workshop and acquiring the anticipated number of participants. (See chapter 7 for details about promoting workshops.)

Step 4: Prepare the e-mail message for promoting the workshop.

Send out the promotional e-mail (see the sidebar) to prospective interested parties between September 1 and September 30.

E-MAIL MESSAGE TO PROMOTE SCENARIO 1 WORKSHOP

Subject line: INVITATION: Collaborating with Strangers for Mini-grant Communications Projects Workshop, October 1, 2:30 to 4:30 p.m., CJC room 100

Hey, Stranger,
Looking for a way to combine forces with others who are interested in communications research and service projects? Join us for this dynamic interchange of people, interests, and knowledge.

The Collaborating with Strangers for Mini-grant Communications Projects workshop will connect students and faculty during a series of three-minute speed-meetings. You'll walk away with more resources, solutions, and creative ideas than you could have ever imagined.

> **When:** Wednesday, October 1, 2:30 to 4:30 p.m.
> **Where:** College of Journalism and Communications, conference room 100
> Refreshments will be served.

For more information and the registration link, contact John Smith at jsmith@xyzlibrary.edu.

Seats are limited. Please register if you are interested or pass this on to other interested people.

Sponsored by the XYZ University Library, the Communications Student Association, and the College of Journalism and Communications.

Step 5: Prepare e-mail message for confirming registration.

The purpose of registration is to estimate the number of people who will attend, to gather e-mail addresses for correspondence, and, in this case, to learn about the diversity of the disciplines represented by participants. There is no actual registration verification during the workshop. Anyone should be able to attend even if he or she did not register in advance. See the sidebar for a sample message.

E-MAIL MESSAGE TO CONFIRM SCENARIO 1 WORKSHOP REGISTRATION

Subject line: RE: ORIENTATION: Collaborating with Strangers for Mini-grant Communications Projects

We're excited you will be joining us for Collaborating with Strangers for Mini-grant Communications Projects.

> **When:** Wednesday, October 1, 2:30 to 4:30 p.m.
> **Where:** College of Journalism and Communications, conference room 100

Please read this brief orientation: When you arrive, you will receive a profile card with the questions listed below. You may prepare answers in advance, if you like. The more detailed your answers to these questions are, the more you will benefit from the workshop. But don't worry if you don't have all the answers—just come and enjoy the experience!

1. What is your current research or service project interest and why are you passionate about this work?
2. What recent collaborative projects have you been involved in and what was your role?
3. What are your skills and strengths?
4. What networks, associations, or other groups do you participate in?
5. What is one thing most people don't know about you?

Refreshments will be provided. If you are interested in learning what past "strangers" had to say about these workshops, check this out: <link>. [This comment assumes that you have gathered testimonials from previously conducted workshops and that these are available online.] Some space is still available, so feel free to encourage your peers or classmates to attend.

The CoLAB team is looking forward to hosting this collaborative and creative experience. We can't wait to meet you!

If you don't have the resources (or time) to create a CoLAB website from scratch but want something more engaging than a PDF to share workshop content, try drafting an online flipbook using this digital publishing platform: https://issuu.com. You can sign up for the free version and create a customized "magazine" based on a variety of attractive, user-friendly templates. Photographs, profile-signs, contact information, and Idea Board responses can be easily uploaded and shared.

When creating the profile-sign template, you may want to consider adding a social media question so participants can share Twitter, LinkedIn, or Instagram handles. Connecting with professional colleagues on social media can be a powerful networking tool for creating dynamic ongoing relationships. In CoLAB Workshops that feature a particular theme, like Sustainability or Big Data, creating a Facebook group will allow participants to continue their conversations in an informal digital space.

Step 6: Plan for workshop information to be shared via a website.

The CoLAB team works with library IT (information technology) staff to develop a website with pages devoted to hosting the following information: (1) scanned profile-signs that are matched up with each participant's headshot along with individual e-mail addresses (this information should be password protected), (2) photos taken during the workshop, (3) feedback provided during the Idea Boards activity, and (4) evaluation results.

Step 7: Organize supplies necessary for the workshop.

Design and print, on 8.5" × 14" legal-size card stock, blank profile-sign templates (see figure 2.3) that include the five profile questions developed during the planning meeting with the professor. Add space for the participant's first name, a box for each participant's workshop number, hometown, home department or area of study, and boxes to check indicating whether the participant is a faculty member, graduate student, or undergraduate student. Include space on the back of the profile-sign for participants to share the workshop date as well as their names and e-mail addresses and brief instructions about the major workshop steps: preparing the profile-sign, completing the permission form, participating in speed-meetings, and completing the postworkshop survey. The postworkshop survey should also be printed on the back of the profile-sign. Other supplies include a blank checklist with space for writing down participant numbers and correlating notes or reminders about ideas from speed-meeting conversations, name tags to be used for participant numbers (not their names), Sharpie fine-point markers, flipchart paper, 3" × 3" Post-it notes, and safety pins.

Step 8: Create workshop agenda.

Prepare an agenda for the workshop that includes time calculations, similar to that shown in table 4.2.

Step 9: Plan CoLAB team roles.

The team assigns its members to each of the following roles for the workshop session: (1) one or two members to greet and orient each participant; (2) a member to distribute supplies as participants enter the room, and to prevent participants from leaving without first returning their completed profile-signs, evaluation surveys, and markers, if they want to leave early; (3) a presenter of the PowerPoint material (see page 59); (4) a bell ringer to time conversations using a smartphone or stopwatch; and (5) two members with their own completed profile-signs to serve as "alternate participants" who are ready to jump into the speed-meeting process when there aren't enough available

TABLE 4.2

AGENDA FOR COLLABORATING WITH STRANGERS FOR MINI-GRANT COMMUNICATIONS PROJECTS CoLAB WORKSHOP

TIME	ACTIVITY
1:45 to 2:15	Participants arrive and receive a profile-sign, fine-point black (Sharpie) marker, and workshop number label. They complete their profile-sign information and have their headshots taken.
2:15 to 2:45	• Participants arriving late continue to complete the previous step. • The communications professor introduces facilitators, describes how to apply for Communications Project Mini-grant funding, and thanks workshop sponsors, including the CoLAB team. • A member of the CoLAB team gives a PowerPoint presentation. (The detailed contents of the presentation appear later in chapter 4, beginning on page 59.)
2:15 to 2:45	• Participants are instructed to raise their right hands and repeat the facilitator's instruction: "I promise to move when I hear the bell." The facilitator explains why moving to a new participant when the bell rings is so important to keeping the process moving and organized. • Participants are instructed that during the speed-meeting process they can either stay seated or stand, whichever is more comfortable. • The speed-meeting process begins with everyone finding a partner. The facilitators should be prepared in advance with extra "participants" who can jump into and out of the process as necessary, depending on whether there is an odd or even number of participants at any given time or if participants forget to move when the bell is rung, so everyone has a different partner to meet during each round.
3:45 to 3:55	Participants are instructed that the final speed-meeting conversation has occurred and to take a seat. Facilitators post three flipchart sheets on the conference room walls, boards, or easels with these three headings: (1) What synergies did you discover? (2) What things did you learn? (3) What are your next steps? These are called Idea Boards. Each participant is given a stack of ten 3" × 3" Post-it notes. Participants are instructed to write as many answers to the questions as possible, one answer per Post-it. Participants are asked to place their Post-it note responses on the appropriate Idea Board.
3:55 to 4:00	Participants are instructed to complete the evaluation survey and to return Sharpies and profile-signs along with the evaluation. A facilitator shares information about the follow-up e-mail message that all participants will receive, which will include a link to view the profile-signs, contact information, and Idea Board comments.

A QUICK TIP

If you plan to take headshots for online follow-up, you may want to promote this as an opportunity for participants to have a professional photo taken. If you don't have an internal photographer, find out if your college or sponsoring organization can provide a photographer who is willing to "work" the event.

strangers for pairing up. Team members will be able to fill more than one of these roles, if necessary. When the presentation and speed-meetings have finished, the team will need to regroup to assist with the Idea Boards activity, distribute Post-it notes and assist with getting feedback notes delivered to the Idea Boards. Before participants leave, the entire team is involved with gathering profile-signs/evaluation surveys, markers, and Idea Board content.

FIGURE 4.1

FLOWCHART FOR SCENARIO 1–PREWORKSHOP ACTIVITIES

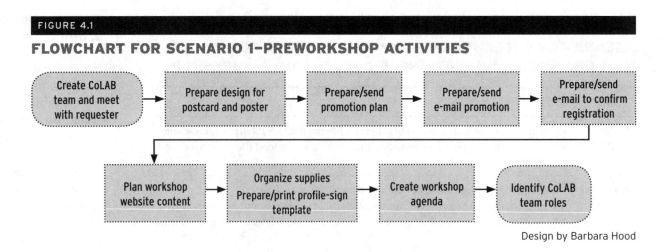

Design by Barbara Hood

Day-of-Workshop Activities for Scenario 1

In this scenario, the workshop begins at 2:30 p.m. and ends at 4:30 p.m.

FIGURE 4.2

FLOOR PLAN FOR SCENARIO 1–ON-CAMPUS SPACE
(NOT IN A LIBRARY)

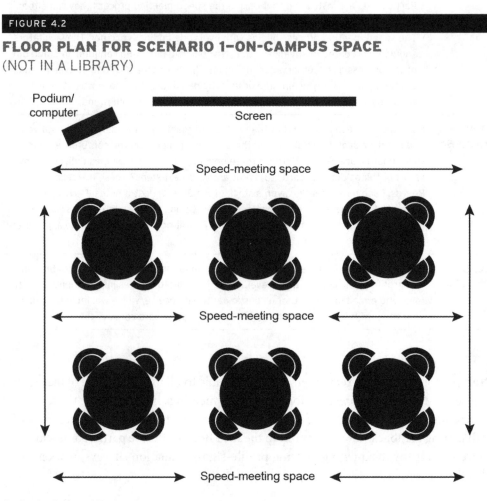

Design by Barbara Hood

Step 10: Dispense instructions and supplies to participants.

As participants arrive, regardless of how early, they will want to get started writing out their profile-sign information. Give each participant one profile-sign, one number label to wear for the headshot, and one fine-point black marker. Some participants will have print copies of their answers to the profile-sign questions, so have some scissors and tape available so they can attach them to their profile-signs. This works as long as the text is 16-point font or larger. Participants should be oriented about when and where to get their headshot photographs taken.

CoLAB PARTICIPANTS RECEIVING SUPPLIES AND COMPLETING PROFILE-SIGNS

Photo by Barbara Hood

VERBAL ORIENTATION FOR SCENARIO 1 WORKSHOP PARTICIPANTS AS THEY ARRIVE

Here you have your profile-sign and your participant number is [5]. Wearing this label will help others identify you by number rather than name and will be used to keep track of your headshot and your profile-sign information. Please use the marker to answer these questions with clear handwriting so others will easily be able to read your answers quickly. Whenever you see that the photographer has space available to take your headshot, feel free to stop preparing your sign and go and get your photo taken. Headshots and profile information will be posted online via a password-protected site.

Step 11: Take headshots of each participant.

As participants begin preparing their signs, they are offered opportunities to have their pictures taken to be included on the password-protected website. The number assigned to each participant is used to track the individual headshots. Those choosing not to have their photo taken will write "NP" at the top of the sign to indicate that no photo was taken to accompany the profile-sign information.

FIGURE 4.4

HEADSHOT TAKEN OF A PARTICIPANT FOR ONLINE FOLLOW-UP

Photo by Bess de Farber

Step 12: Participants complete their profile-signs.

This takes an average of ten to fifteen minutes. Music can be softly playing in the background. Even if participants arrive late, they should be welcomed to the workshop, provided with the supplies and orientation, instructed to complete their profile-signs, and encouraged to get their photographs taken. They can be included in the workshop even if they have missed the presentation and some of the speed-meeting rounds.

FIGURE 4.5

CoLAB PARTICIPANTS COMPLETING PROFILE-SIGNS

Photo by Barbara Hood

Step 13: Present the PowerPoint material.

Even if not all of the participants have arrived, begin the presentation and encourage participants to continue completing their profile-signs. Present information related to the history of CoLAB Workshops (see chapter 2), workshop objectives, methods to combine forces with others, tips on ways to develop creativity, and instructions for participating in speed-meetings. The following content for these slides provides the framework for your CoLAB Workshop presentation. (For a sample PowerPoint slide show, visit http://ufdc.ufl.edu//IR00008442/00001.)

SLIDE 1
Use the workshop promotional graphic icon from the postcard or poster; include workshop date, team members' names, and the name(s) of the sponsor.

SLIDE 2
Introduce and show a short video clip from Steven Johnson's TED Talk "Where Good Ideas Come From" (www.ted.com/talks/steven_johnson_where _good_ideas_come_from?language=en).

SLIDE 3
Share information about CoLAB Planning Series Workshops: background and history, basic principles, and the role of libraries in presenting CoLAB Workshops.

SLIDE 4

Present the workshop objectives: (1) practice conversing with strangers, (2) identify new resources and learn from new people, (3) practice noticing commonalities and differences in profile information, and (4) spark ideas, solutions, or access to new information.

SLIDE 5

Review the five ways to combine forces with others: cooperation, coordination, collaboration, mentorship/coaching, and friendship.

Note: For the next three slides, use the previously discussed definitions established by Wilder Foundation researchers (see page 21).

SLIDE 6

Define cooperation, and give an example of this type of activity.

SLIDE 7

Define coordination, and give an example of this type of activity.

SLIDE 8

Define collaboration, and give an example of this type of activity.

SLIDE 9

Inform participants about the four basic requirements to increasing one's engagement in asset-based partnerships:

- Know your own assets.
- Learn about your colleagues' and friends' assets.
- Learn about your institution's assets.
- Practice combining and leveraging these assets when opportunities arise.

SLIDE 10

Share information about ways to encourage creativity, such as the following:

- Increase face-to-face conversations with strangers.
- Avoid routine.
- Seek criticism—what can you do better?
- Invite "new" people to join teams with folks you already work with.
- Be curious, disadvantaged, open to giving and receiving, and allocate time to ideate.
- Avoid saying "no" to new opportunities.
- Revise and reuse others' ideas.

SLIDE 11

Share a short humorous video on ideating or on any of the concepts listed on slide 10.

SLIDE 12

Provide speed-meeting instructions:

- Find a partner.
- Locate/check the participant's number and write it on your checklist so you will remember to whom you spoke.

- Read your partner's sign.
- Converse for three minutes.
- Feel free to sit or stand or move to a quiet area.
- Listen for instructions throughout the workshop.
- When you hear the bell, say an immediate good-bye and find a new partner.
- Take notes during the conversations as reminders (there's no need to capture contact information).

Step 14: Demonstrate the proper position and use of the profile-sign.

Demonstrate how to pin the profile-sign to the upper chest so that others can easily read it, or suggest that holding the sign is possible but doesn't allow participants to write notes or move around with their hands free.

Step 15: Administer oath and instruct participants to find partners.

Have participants raise their right hands to repeat this facetious oath: "I promise . . . [*participants repeat*] to move . . . [*participants repeat*] when I hear the bell . . . [*participants repeat*]." Tell participants to find partners and to remember to read their partners' profile-signs before discussing anything.

A QUICK TIP

You can offer participants the option of using a ribbon or a lanyard, instead of a safety pin, to loop the sign around their necks.

FIGURE 4.6

FACILITATOR ASKING PARTICIPANTS TO PROMISE TO MOVE TO A NEW PARTNER WHEN THE BELL RINGS

Photo by Barbara Hood

Step 16: Once everyone has partnered, begin the speed-meeting rounds.

Start the stopwatch when everyone has found a partner. Have a team member participate if there is an odd number of participants. Ring the bell after four minutes to end the first meeting, and keep ringing the bell until most participants have moved to new partners. End the next speed-meeting at three minutes forty-five seconds, but start again after everyone has found a new partner. Continue decreasing the time allotment by increments of fifteen seconds each round until you reach three minutes per round, and continue this pattern with three-minute rounds until the allotted time for speed-meetings has expired.

Step 17: End speed-meetings.

Announce that the speed-meetings have ended and request that participants take their seats.

Step 18: Distribute materials and explain instructions for the Idea Board activity.

Have some team members distribute a stack of ten 3" × 3" Post-it notes to each participant, while other team members are affixing three flipchart pages—Idea Boards—to the wall, each of which displays one of these questions:

1. What synergies or connections did you discover?
2. What did you learn?
3. What are your next steps?

Instruct participants to write as many answers to these questions as they choose, with one answer per Post-it. Have participants affix their answers to the Idea Boards, or have the team members assist by gathering answers and affixing them to the appropriate Idea Boards, thus allowing participants to continue writing more answers. Inform participants that all the responses will be posted (anonymously) to the CoLAB Workshop website.

Step 19: Have participants fill out the evaluation survey, contact information, and permission forms and encourage them to follow up with contacts made and with strangers they didn't have a chance to meet.

Instruct participants to complete the evaluation surveys, contact information, and permission forms (for sharing photographs) located on the back of their profile-signs and to return their profile-signs and markers. Provide information about the follow-up e-mail message, which will include links to the profile-signs, with their corresponding headshots and contact information, as well as transcripts of the Idea Board results and photographs taken during the speed-meeting process. Wish all the participants good luck in their lives, and encourage them to follow up with other CoLABers, both those they have met and those they have not yet met.

FIGURE 4.7

PARTICIPANT AFFIXING RESPONSES TO IDEA BOARD

Photo by Barbara Hood

FIGURE 4.8

FLOWCHART FOR SCENARIO 1–DAY-OF-WORKSHOP ACTIVITIES

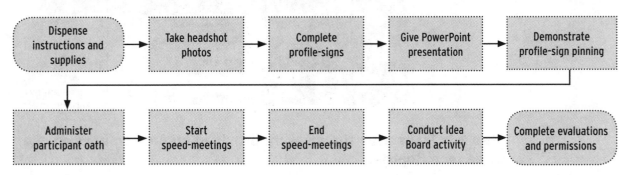

Design by Barbara Hood

Postworkshop Activities for Scenario 1

Step 20: Verify evaluation surveys and permission forms.

Check to see that the evaluation surveys and permission forms have been completed. Follow up by e-mail to contact those who did not complete this information.

Step 21: Process the profile-signs and headshots for online access.

Scan profile-signs to PDF format (either in one large file or as separate files for each participant) and crop headshots using photo-editing software, such as Photoshop.

Some participants will choose not to share their headshots publicly and/or not to allow publication of photographs taken during the session in which they appear. The CoLAB team should tag these profile-signs to ensure participants' requests are being met.

Step 22: Match headshots with their appropriate profile-signs.

This is achieved by electronically combining files related to the number in each participant's headshot with the corresponding number that appears on the profile-sign.

FIGURE 4.9

PARTICIPANT HEADSHOT AND PROFILE-SIGN ON WEBSITE

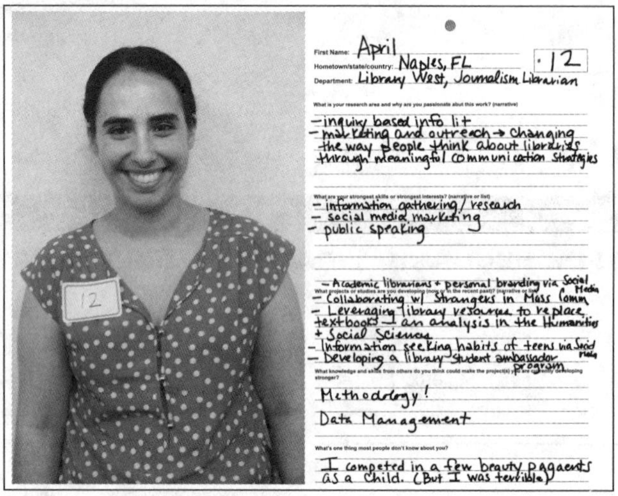

Document by April Hines

Step 23: Transcribe the answers provided by participants on the three Idea Boards.

Allocate sufficient time to complete the transcription as sometimes the handwriting is difficult to decipher. Also, verify that the answers are appropriate for each question and weren't mistakenly affixed to the wrong Idea Board.

Step 24: Make workshop materials accessible to participants.

Load files to a website—or create an online flipbook or one comprehensive PDF—for sharing workshop profiles and Idea Board responses.

Step 25: Prepare and send postworkshop e-mail message to participants and the communications professor.

See the sidebar for a sample e-mail message.

E-MAIL MESSAGE TO SHARE SCENARIO 1 POST-CoLAB WORKSHOP INFORMATION

Subject line: RE: CoLAB Workshop Follow-Up Information

Dear CoLABer,

Thank you for participating in the library's CoLAB Workshop, Collaborating with Strangers on Mini-grants in Communications Projects. The CoLAB team has organized information from participants who agreed to share their profile-signs and headshots. You can access the page here: <link>. Profile-signs have been organized in participant numerical order, and you will find contact information on the signs as well. We encourage you to connect with one or more workshop participants who attended the CoLAB. [*Optional*] You will receive a follow-up survey in several weeks as the CoLAB project team continues to gather information about the impact of this workshop . . . including connections and collaborations.

Website CoLAB Connections:

We have organized information provided by participants who agreed to share their profiles within a secure webpage. You can access the page here: <link>.

Instructions on how to use the webpage:

The above link leads to a password-protected page. Use your access ID and password to log in.

- You will see the profile of participant 1.
- You can use the thumbnails located below the profiles to select and view any of the desired profiles.
- You can find the contact e-mail address at the bottom of the profile.
- To enlarge the view of the profile, click "View Larger Image," found below the profile.

Posted Workshop Idea Boards:

Check out the ideas shared on the CoLAB Idea Boards here: <link>.

Posted CoLAB Workshop Photographs:

You can view workshop photos here: <link>.

Keep checking the Collaborating with Strangers home page for upcoming workshop topics and dates. We hope to see you at future CoLAB Workshops. Please feel free to e-mail your questions or feedback.

Step 26: Analyze evaluation surveys and in-person observations, and prepare an evaluation report.

In this scenario, a CoLAB team member scans the completed surveys on the back side of the profile-signs and develops a template for analyzing the participants' responses, including some data found on the profile-signs about hometown, area of study, and type of participant (i.e., undergraduate student, graduate student, or faculty). The team analyzes the template data and combines the analysis with observations provided by the neutral observer who attended the workshop for producing the evaluation report.

Step 27: Share the evaluation report and workshop results.

You can post these to the CoLAB Workshop's website or send these to the participants through a link.

FIGURE 4.10

FLOWCHART FOR SCENARIO 1–POSTWORKSHOP ACTIVITIES

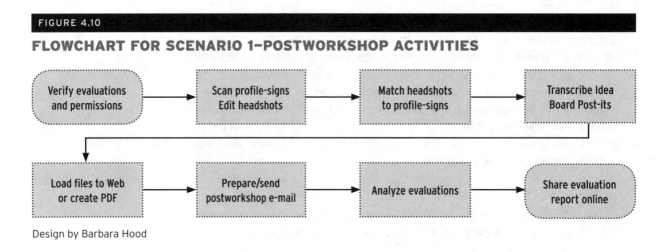

Design by Barbara Hood

Scenario 2: On-Campus Library CoLAB Workshop

Scenarios 1 and 2—and the others shared in this chapter—differ in that the workshop team will have new considerations and constraints to manage in each of the workshops. Several of the steps, as might be expected, are similar among all of the scenarios. This scenario description features the steps for facilitating an internal CoLAB Workshop designed to serve faculty and staff in a large academic library. The library CoLAB team wants to remove the barriers that prevent academic librarians and other staff from knowing about one another's research interests, projects, and skills. The idea to present this CoLAB was suggested during a faculty assembly meeting as part of a discussion on the new requirements for performing research within the tenure and promotion process. With this in mind, the team tests the idea about presenting a CoLAB titled Collaborating with Strangers: Connecting through Research Interests with Library Faculty and Staff.

Other colleagues in the library share enthusiasm about having a structured process for learning more about their co-workers. Another consideration related to this scenario is that because of the many retirements, the library has hired seven new librarians and staff in the past year. Time is a precious commodity for those who work in libraries or other service-based organizations. But the consensus is that two hours is a reasonable amount of time to spend learning about their colleagues' research interests and skills. Beyond increasing their knowledge of their colleagues' research interests, additional benefits for those who choose to participate in this particular CoLAB Workshop include the following:

- Having the opportunity to converse with newly hired employees, thus accelerating the integration process for building a sense of community with new recruits
- Providing access to information about skills and networks that may relate to supporting others' research or projects
- Reducing the time required to meet one-on-one with individual librarians, each of whom is pursuing different research interests and has innumerable resources and professional assets to share that possibly will be invaluable to colleagues

Preworkshop Activities for Scenario 2

Step 1: Create a CoLAB team and plan the workshop.

In this scenario, the CoLAB team consists of library research group leaders. They create a title for the workshop (if not previously finalized), set the date(s) and time, choose the space, and decide on refreshments.

For this workshop, the title will be Collaborating on Research Projects with Library Faculty and Staff. The workshop will take place in the multipurpose meeting room, from 10:00 a.m. to 1:00 p.m. on December 15, with lunch following the workshop.

Step 2: Seek the necessary approvals for reserving workshop space and secure funding or an in-kind donation for refreshments.

The team members decide to apply for support from a sponsor as a means for providing lunch. They submit an online application to Chipotle (http://chipotle.com/email-us#philanthropy) six weeks in advance and later receive an approval to receive lunch for forty participants.

Step 3: Prepare the list of questions for the profile-signs.

The team decides on the following questions: (1) What is the research project you are currently working on and why are you passionate about this project? If you don't have a research project, what research interests are you considering for a future project

A QUICK TIP

If you are planning a CoLAB that is more than three hours long or falls during lunch- or dinnertime, you will need to provide more substantial refreshments beyond cookies and drinks. Preordered deli sandwiches, chips, fruit, and dessert will often feed a great number of people for the least cost. Try serving food either before the workshop (participants can eat during the initial presentation) or after the speed-meeting process when everyone is more familiar with one another and ready to chat and socialize.

and why is this topic important to you? (2) What other projects have you worked on, including nonresearch projects, in the past three years? (3) What are your strongest skills? (4) What networks or organizations do you belong to? (5) What is one thing most people don't know about you?

Step 4: Prepare the e-mail message for promoting the workshop, and set up a registration system.

Use the registration system to determine the number of people who plan to participate and also to gather contact information for each registrant. See the sidebar for a sample promotional message.

E-MAIL MESSAGE TO PROMOTE SCENARIO 2 WORKSHOP

Subject line: RE: INVITATION: Collaboration Workshop, December 15, 10:00 a.m. to 1:00 p.m., Multipurpose Room

Hey, Library Staff Member,
Are you looking for a way to combine forces with others who are engaged in library-related research projects? Join us for this dynamic interchange of people, interests, and knowledge.

The Collaborating on Research Projects with Library Faculty and Staff workshop will connect the library participants during a series of three-minute speed-meetings. You'll walk away with more resources, solutions, and creative ideas than you could have ever imagined.

> **When:** Friday, December 15, 10:00 a.m. to 1:00 p.m.
> **Where:** Library Multipurpose Room
> Lunch will be provided.

For more information and a registration link, contact Mary Johnson at mjohnson@xyzlibrary.edu.

Please register if you are interested so that we will know how many participants to expect.

Sponsor: Chipotle Restaurants

Step 5: Prepare e-mail message to confirm participation.

See the sidebar on page 69 for a sample e-mail message.

Step 6: Plan for workshop information to be shared.

In this scenario, the team plans to create a PDF that includes images of all the profile-signs.

E-MAIL MESSAGE CONFIRMING SCENARIO 2 WORKSHOP PARTICIPATION

Subject line: RE: ORIENTATION: Collaboration Workshop, December 15, 10:00 a.m. to 1:00 p.m., Multipurpose Room

We're excited that you will be joining us for Collaborating on Research Projects with Library Faculty and Staff.

> **When:** Friday, December 15, 10:00 a.m. to 1:00 p.m.
> **Where:** Library Multipurpose Room

Please read this brief orientation: When you arrive, you will receive a profile-sign with the questions listed below. You may prepare answers in advance, if you like. The more detailed the answers to these questions, the more you will benefit from the workshop. But don't worry if you don't have all of the answers—just come and enjoy the experience!

1. What is your current research or service project interest, and why are you passionate about this work?
2. What recent collaborative projects have you been involved in, and what was your role?
3. What are your skills, strengths, and interests?
4. What networks, associations, or other groups do you participate in?
5. What is one thing most people don't know about you?

Lunch will be provided. If you are interested in learning what past "strangers" had to say about these workshops, check this out: <link>. [This comment assumes that you have gathered testimonials from previously conducted workshops and that these are available online.]

The CoLAB team is looking forward to hosting this collaborative and creative experience. We can't wait to learn more about you!

Step 7: Organize supplies necessary for the workshop.

Design and print, on 8.5" × 14" legal-size card stock, blank profile-sign templates and include the five profile questions developed by the team. Add space for each participant's first name and a box for each participant's workshop number, hometown, and library department. The back of the profile-sign should include space for participants to share the workshop date as well as their names and e-mail addresses and brief instructions about the major workshop steps: preparing profile-signs, completing permissions, engaging in speed-meetings, and completing the postworkshop survey. Other supplies include a blank checklist with space for writing participant numbers and correlating notes or reminders about ideas from speed-meeting conversations, name tags to be used for participant numbers (not their names), Sharpie fine-point markers, flipchart paper, 3" × 3" Post-it notes, and safety pins. The postworkshop survey also should be included on the back of the profile-signs.

Step 8: Create workshop agenda.

The workshop agenda should be similar to that shown in table 4.3.

TABLE 4.3

AGENDA FOR COLLABORATING ON RESEARCH PROJECTS WITH LIBRARY FACULTY AND STAFF CoLAB WORKSHOP

TIME	ACTIVITY
9:45 to 10:15	Participants arrive and receive profile-signs, fine-point black markers, and workshop number labels.
10:15 to 10:35	• Participants arriving late continue to complete the previous steps. • A member of the CoLAB team gives a PowerPoint presentation. [The detailed contents of the presentation were described previously, beginning on page 59.]
10:35 to 11:45	• Participants are instructed to raise their right hands and repeat the facilitator's instruction: "I promise to move when I hear the bell." The facilitator explains why moving to a new partner is so important to keeping the process moving and organized. • Participants are instructed to stay seated or stand, whichever is more comfortable. • The process begins with everyone finding a partner. The facilitators should be prepared in advance with extra "participants" who can jump into and out of the process as necessary, depending on whether there is an odd or even number of participants at any given time or if participants forget to move when the bell is rung.
11:45 to 12:15	Participants are instructed that the final speed-meeting conversation has occurred and they should take a seat. Facilitators post three flipchart sheets—Idea Boards—on the conference wall with these three headings: (1) What synergies did you discover? (2) What things did you learn? (3) What are your next steps? Each participant is given a stack of ten 3" × 3" Post-it notes. Participants are instructed to write as many answers to the questions as possible, one answer per Post-it. Participants are asked to place their Post-it notes on the appropriate Idea Board.
12:15 to 12:50	Lunch is served. A facilitator encourages participants to freely mingle with one another to follow up on possible projects or common interests or to meet those they didn't have a chance to meet during the speed-meetings. Ring the bell to signal the end of this free time.
12:50 to 1:00	Participants are instructed to complete the evaluation form information and to return the Sharpies, profile-signs, and evaluations. A facilitator shares information about the follow-up e-mail message that all participants will receive, which will include a link to view the profile-signs, contact information, and Idea Board comments.

Step 9: Plan team member roles.

Do this in the same manner as described under Step 9 for Scenario 1 (see page 54).

(see page 54)

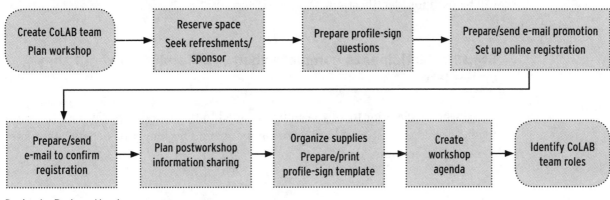

FIGURE 4.11

FLOWCHART FOR SCENARIO 2–PREWORKSHOP ACTIVITIES

Design by Barbara Hood

Day-of-Workshop Activities for Scenario 2

In this scenario, the workshop begins at 10:00 a.m. and ends at 1:00 p.m.

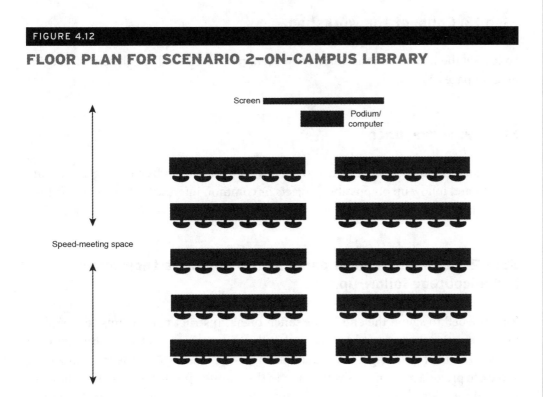

FIGURE 4.12

FLOOR PLAN FOR SCENARIO 2–ON-CAMPUS LIBRARY

Design by Barbara Hood

Step 10: Dispense instructions and supplies to participants.

Follow the procedure as described in Scenario 1, Step 10 (see page 57).

Since the participants involved in Scenario 2 generally will be expected to be working in the same physical proximity—they all work for the same organization—typically it will not be necessary to take headshots for this type of workshop. Number labels also will not be necessary; instead, the participant names appearing on the profile-signs will be used for identification.

Step 11: Participants complete their profile-signs, even if they arrive late.

Those who arrive prior to 11:15 can be included in this workshop session. (The team should decide at what time in the workshop it would no longer be beneficial for late-comers to be accommodated.)

Step 12: Present the PowerPoint material.

Follow the process outlined in Scenario 1, Step 13 (beginning on page 59). Even if not all of the participants have arrived, begin the presentation and encourage everyone to continue completing their profile-signs as needed.

Step 13: Conduct the workshop.

Follow all the instructions as outlined in Scenario 1, Step 14 through Step 18 (beginning on page 61).

Step 19: Serve lunch.

A facilitator instructs participants to use the lunch break to freely mingle with one another and follow up on possible projects or common interests or to meet those they didn't have a chance to meet.

Step 20: End lunch, have participants complete their forms, and encourage follow-up.

Ring the bell to signal the end of the lunch break. Instruct participants to complete their evaluation surveys and to ensure that their names and contact information are included on the profile-signs. Also share that an e-mail message will be sent out within a week to provide participants with a link to the scanned profile-signs so that they can view information about those they did not meet, as well as those they met, to make it easier for them to follow up after the workshop.

FIGURE 4.13

SPEED-MEETINGS DURING A CoLAB WITH LIBRARIANS FROM MULTIPLE BRANCHES OF THE SAME LIBRARY SYSTEM

Photo by Barbara Hood

FIGURE 4.14

FLOWCHART FOR SCENARIO 2–DAY-OF-WORKSHOP ACTIVITIES

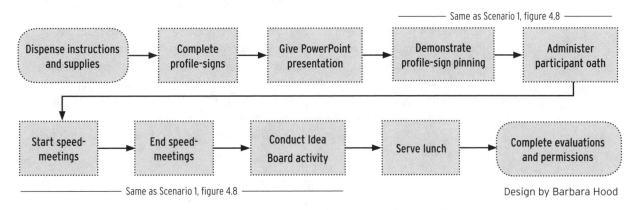

Design by Barbara Hood

Postworkshop Activities for Scenario 2

Step 21: Verify evaluation surveys and permission forms.

Check to see that evaluation surveys have been completed and that you have permission from each participant to share his or her profile-sign with only the other workshop participants. You also can offer a provision for participants to grant their permission to share profile-signs with everyone in the academic library as a means of inspiring even more collaborative initiatives.

73

Step 22: Process the profile-signs.

Scan profile-signs in alphabetical order by last name into one large PDF, and make sure contact information for each participant is visible.

Step 23: Transcribe the responses provided for the three Idea Boards.

Verify that the answers are appropriate for each question and weren't mistakenly affixed to the wrong Idea Board. Try to complete the transcription soon after the workshop so that the PDF of these responses is ready for participants prior to sending the follow-up e-mail message in the next step.

Step 24: Prepare and send postworkshop e-mail message to participants.

See the sidebar for a sample message.

E-MAIL MESSAGE TO SHARE SCENARIO 2 POST-CoLAB WORKSHOP INFORMATION

Subject line: RE: CoLAB Workshop Follow-Up Information

Dear CoLABer,
Thank you for participating in the library's CoLAB Workshop. The CoLAB team has organized information from participants who agreed to share their profiles. You can access the page here: <link>. Profile-signs have been organized in participant-number order, and you will find contact information on the signs as well. We encourage you to connect with one or more workshop participants who attended the CoLAB. You will receive a follow-up survey in several weeks as the CoLAB project team continues to gather information about the impact of this workshop, including new connections and partnerships.

Ideas shared during workshop:
Check out the ideas shared on the CoLAB Idea Boards here: <link>.

CoLAB Workshop photos:
You can view workshop photographs here: <link>.

We hope to see you at future CoLAB Workshops. Please feel free to e-mail your questions or feedback.

Thanks again for CoLABing with us!
The CoLAB Workshop Team

Step 25: Compile and analyze evaluation surveys, in-person observations, and other feedback, and prepare an evaluation report.

In this scenario, a CoLAB team member scans the completed surveys on the back side of the profile-signs and develops a template for analyzing the participants' responses. The team analyzes the template data and combines the analysis with observations provided by the neutral observer who attended the workshop for producing the evaluation report.

Step 26: Share the evaluation report and workshop results through an e-mail message to all participants.

By sharing the evaluation report with participants (library staff), the CoLAB team builds buy-in for making CoLABs an ongoing program of the library, not just a one-time workshop.

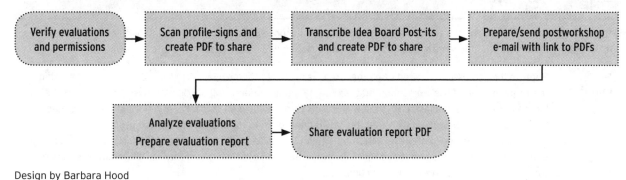

FIGURE 4.15

FLOWCHART FOR SCENARIO 2—POSTWORKSHOP ACTIVITIES

Verify evaluations and permissions → Scan profile-signs and create PDF to share → Transcribe Idea Board Post-its and create PDF to share → Prepare/send postworkshop e-mail with link to PDFs

Analyze evaluations / Prepare evaluation report → Share evaluation report PDF

Design by Barbara Hood

Scenario 3: Classroom CoLAB Workshop

Presenting a CoLAB Workshop in a classroom setting can be an excellent way to quickly orient students who previously have not engaged together. The backstory to this scenario is that the CoLAB team has been asked to present a workshop for students enrolled in the Entrepreneurship Business course. The professor teaching the course has explained that these undergraduate students come from many different disciplines and typically do not know anyone else in the class. Her goal is to allow students to participate in a CoLAB Workshop where all twenty-eight students will meet one another and then form teams of between two and four members to produce business plans for creating new companies that may or may not be actualized in the future, as their final course project.

The professor sees that a CoLAB Workshop may be the best vehicle for completing this team formation process, particularly for the benefit derived from minimizing conflicts that may arise when teams are formed by a professor who doesn't know the students or their interests. Other benefits for students in this workshop include the following:

- Revealing their colleagues' business interests and extant skills at the outset of the course to open up new possibilities for collaboration or supportive relationships
- Learning about students' interests outside their coursework for developing friendships
- Sharing information about hometowns to determine other possibilities for connections related to common geographical location

Preworkshop Activities for Scenario 3

Step 1: Create a CoLAB team and meet with the business professor.

Use the agenda in table 4.4 for guiding the meeting discussion.

TABLE 4.4

AGENDA FOR AN HOUR MEETING WITH THE ENTREPRENEURSHIP PROFESSOR

TIME	ACTIVITY
10 minutes	Give an overview of a typical CoLAB Workshop, its purpose of connecting strangers with one another's assets, its possible length, and options for workshop agenda activities.
5 minutes	Confirm the professor's desired outcomes to have students themselves form their own entrepreneurship teams by the end of the workshop and that twenty-eight students will participate. Also confirm that the length of the available classroom time will be sufficient to allow all of the twenty-eight students to meet their classmates (27 students x 4 minutes = 108 minutes + 45 minutes for preparing profile-signs and completing the PowerPoint presentation = 153 minutes). Add another thirty minutes for self-selecting student entrepreneurship teams and for completing evaluation surveys. The grand total of 183 minutes means the workshop will require three hours to complete.
40 minutes	Once the length of the workshop has been decided, then through a consensus-building conversation led by the facilitators, develop answers to the following questions: • Other than the facilitators, who will present at the workshop? (Answer: The entrepreneurship professor will provide brief opening remarks, including an introduction of the CoLAB team, a description of the team "new business" assignment, and the requirement that by the end of the workshop, everyone will have selected teammates with whom to complete the final project.) • What questions will be used on the profile-signs? (Answer: [1] What type of company would you be interested in forming and why are you passionate about this business venture? [2] What recent collaborative projects have you been involved in and what was your role? [3] What are your skills and strengths related to producing the final company plan document? [4] What networks, associations, or other groups do you participate in? [5] What is one thing most people don't know about you?) • Where will the workshop be presented? (Answer: This workshop will take place in a classroom within the College of Business that features individual seats with attached desks. The room includes a computer, screen, and projector. There is plenty of walking space to accommodate twenty-eight participants as they move from one conversation to another. No room setup is required. The team agrees to visit the classroom prior to the workshop to plan for space usage.) • What date and time will the workshop be presented? (Answer: January 5 from 1:00 to 4:00 p.m.) • How will the workshop be evaluated and by whom? (Answer: A librarian with assessment expertise will design the evaluation plan and instrument and will maintain a neutral observation role during the workshop.) • Who will provide refreshments? (Answer: The College of Business will provide bottled water and cookies.)
5 minutes	Review all of the confirmed decisions and follow-up actions; identify persons responsible for each action to reduce confusion and misunderstandings.

Step 2: Organize the supplies necessary for the workshop.

Design and print, on 8.5" × 14" legal-size paper, blank profile-sign templates and include the five profile questions developed during the planning meeting with the professor. Add space for the participant's first name, a box for each participant's workshop number, hometown, home department or area of study, and boxes to check whether a graduate student or an undergraduate student. On the back of the profile-signs, participants will find space for sharing the workshop date, their names and e-mail addresses; and brief instructions about the major workshop steps: preparing profile-signs, completing the permission form, participating in speed-meetings, and completing the postworkshop survey. Other supplies include a blank checklist with space for writing participant numbers and correlating notes or reminders about ideas from speed-meeting conversations, name tags to be used for participant numbers (not their names), Sharpie fine-point markers, flipchart paper, 3" × 3" Post-it notes, and safety pins. The postworkshop survey also should be located on the back of the profile-signs.

Step 3: Create workshop agenda.

Create an agenda that includes time calculations, similar to the one shown in table 4.5.

A QUICK TIP

Planning a CoLAB with a predefined group, such as a class or student or community organization, removes the steps of recruiting participants and marketing on a large scale. Starting with a built-in audience guarantees participation and expedites the process if you are pressed for time to deliver the workshop.

TABLE 4.5

AGENDA FOR A CLASSROOM CoLAB WORKSHOP

TIME	ACTIVITY
1:00 to 1:10	The entrepreneurship professor introduces the CoLAB team and shares information about the purpose of the workshop, a description of the final business plan project, and the requirement that everyone select teams in which to participate by the end of the workshop. She explains that in the past she has assigned students to teams randomly, but that conflicts had arisen and teams had had trouble completing their business plan projects. Her view is that the CoLAB Workshop will allow students to self-select their teams based on information shared during the workshop. The professor answers questions posed by the students about the process and the business plan project assignment.
1:10 to 1:40	• The team distributes profile-signs, Sharpie markers, number tags, and checklists. Students complete their profile-signs. • A member of the CoLAB team gives a PowerPoint presentation. [The detailed contents of the presentation were described previously in this chapter, beginning on page 59.] • Students are instructed to raise their right hands and repeat the facilitator's instruction: "I promise to move when I hear the bell." The facilitator explains why moving to a new participant is so important to keeping the process moving and organized. • Students are instructed to stay seated or stand, whichever is more comfortable. • The speed-meeting process begins with everyone finding a partner. In the case where there is an odd number of students, a speed-meeting pairing will include three students instead of two.
1:40 to 3:30	Facilitate the speed-meeting process.
3:30 to 4:00	A facilitator announces that the final speed-meeting conversation has occurred. Students are instructed to spend the rest of the time taking a quick break, selecting their business plan teams, and completing the workshop evaluations.

Step 4: Plan CoLAB team roles.

Unlike other scenarios, participants will all meet one another. Because this is a classroom environment, only two facilitators are needed to (1) dispense supplies and assist students in completing their profile-signs, (2) present the CoLAB PowerPoint workshop material, (3) operate the stopwatch and ring the bell for each speed-meeting round, (4) assist when students are finding other students to meet during the speed-meeting rounds, because the goal is for all students to meet one another, and (5) collect the profile-signs with completed evaluation surveys and rosters of business plan team members.

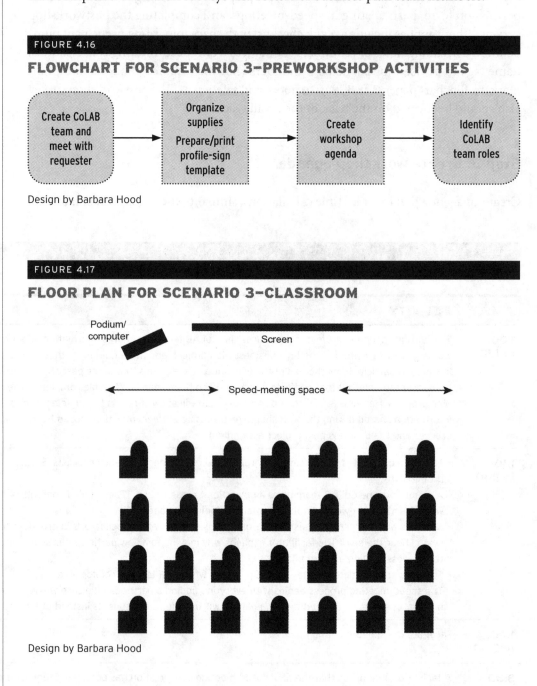

FIGURE 4.16

FLOWCHART FOR SCENARIO 3-PREWORKSHOP ACTIVITIES

Create CoLAB team and meet with requester → Organize supplies / Prepare/print profile-sign template → Create workshop agenda → Identify CoLAB team roles

Design by Barbara Hood

FIGURE 4.17

FLOOR PLAN FOR SCENARIO 3-CLASSROOM

Podium/computer

Screen

Speed-meeting space

Design by Barbara Hood

Day-of-Workshop Activities for Scenario 3

In this scenario, the workshop begins at 1:00 p.m. and ends at 4:00 p.m.

Step 5: Begin the workshop with an introduction and distribute supplies.

The entrepreneurship professor gives an introduction to the workshop participants as facilitators distribute supplies to the students. Students complete their profile-signs.

Step 6: Present the PowerPoint material.

Follow the procedure outlined in Scenario 1, Step 13 (beginning on page 59).

Step 7: Demonstrate the proper position and use of the profile-sign.

Demonstrate how to pin the sign to the chest so that others can easily read it, or suggest that holding the sign is an option but doesn't allow students to take notes or move around with their hands free. Let students know that at any time they need to take a bathroom break, they should let the facilitator know so that partnering accommodations can be facilitated while students are absent from the process.

Step 8: Administer the oath and have participants partner up.

Have participants raise their right hands and repeat this facetious oath: "I promise . . . [*participants repeat*] to move . . . [*participants repeat*] when I hear the bell . . . [*participants repeat*]." Tell participants to find partners and to remember to read their partners' profile-signs before discussing anything.

Step 9: Conduct speed-meetings.

Start the stopwatch when everyone has found a partner. If there is an odd number of students at any time during the speed-meeting process, then one conversation in each three-minute round should take place with three students rather than two. Ring the bell after four minutes to end the first speed-meeting, and keep ringing the bell until most participants have moved to a new partner. End the next speed-meeting at three minutes forty-five seconds, but start again after everyone has found a new partner. Continue decreasing the time allotment by increments of fifteen seconds each round until you reach three minutes per round, and continue this pattern with three-minute rounds until the allotted time for speed-meetings has expired.

A QUICK TIP

If you are conducting a CoLAB in a classroom setting, you will want to skip the headshot portion of the workshop. Furthermore, the Family Educational Rights and Privacy Act (FERPA) regulations prohibit taking photographs of students in a classroom setting. Students naturally will be developing ongoing relationships with their classmates. Taking headshots would be superfluous because the students will be seeing one another in class throughout the semester.

FIGURE 4.18

SPEED-MEETING DURING A CoLAB WITH UNDERGRADUATE STUDENTS

Photo by Barbara Hood

Step 10: End speed-meetings and have participants team up for the business plan project assignment.

When the twenty-seven speed-meeting rounds have been completed or all of the students have met one another (whichever occurs first), instruct students to begin the process of identifying which teams they want to form for completing the business plan project assignment. Suggest that it's best to continue wearing the profile-signs as a means of reminding one another of interests and assets. Instruct students that once the teams have been formed, each team should submit rosters of members and the theme of their collective business plan idea to the professor.

Step 11: Have participants complete evaluation survey.

In this scenario, photographs were not taken, making it unnecessary to include permission forms.

Postworkshop Activities for Scenario 3

Postworkshop activities are minimal for CoLABs that occur in a classroom setting.

FIGURE 4.19

FLOWCHART FOR SCENARIO 3—DAY-OF-WORKSHOP ACTIVITIES

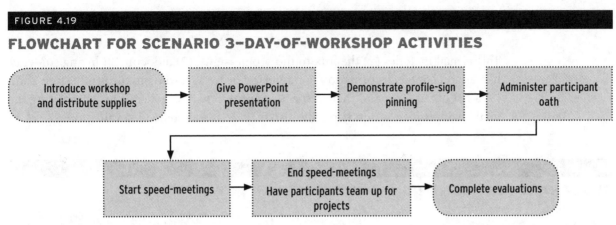

Design by Barbara Hood

Step 12: Verify that evaluation surveys and permission forms are complete.

This step can be completed quickly, immediately following the workshop, so that there is sufficient time to obtain survey information from those who didn't complete these activities during the workshop.

Step 13: Process participants' profile-signs.

Organize profile-signs by participant numbers, to match up with the number tags worn during the session (even though headshots were not taken), and scan to create a PDF. Make sure that the students' first names and contact information are included on their profile-signs.

Step 14: Compile and analyze evaluation surveys and produce an evaluation report.

This step may take a significant amount of time if the CoLAB team lacks in-house assessment experience. If this is the case, the team should identify prospects for acquiring this expertise.

Step 15: Prepare and send an e-mail message to the entrepreneurship professor.

This e-mail should include (1) a link to the profile-signs PDF and (2) an attached evaluation report. Because of FERPA regulations, last name and contact information for each student have been excluded from the profile-signs. Consequently, the professor is responsible for sharing contact information related to each student who participated in the workshop.

Step 16: The professor sends an e-mail message to her students.

This e-mail includes (1) the link to the profile-signs, (2) a document listing students' names and contact information in numerical order according to the profile-signs, and (3) a list of students and their respective entrepreneurship teams for completing the final business plan assignment. She also may decide to share the evaluation report.

FLOWCHART FOR SCENARIO 3–POSTWORKSHOP ACTIVITIES

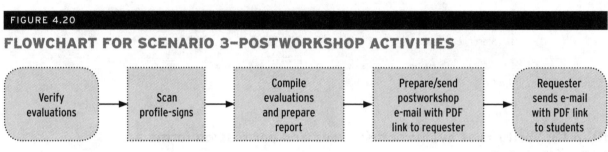

Design by Barbara Hood

Scenario 4: Community CoLAB Workshop in a Public Library

This is the most complex scenario of the four scenarios described in this chapter. It is complex because of the many different types of participants who will be attending. Scenario 4 presents the situation where a community is struggling to resolve a discrete problem of homelessness, namely, barriers to accessing information about available resources. The requester is the community's United Way Agency executive director, who has contacted the local public library director for assistance with providing relevant health care and social service information to those who are homeless. He is requesting the facilitation of a CoLAB Workshop for those agencies serving the homeless and for graduate students who are researching issues related to homelessness.

The participants, each of whom individually has been invited to attend, are directors and program staff employed by a variety of social service and health care providers (forty) plus two representatives from the United Way Agency, and five graduate students and their behavioral sciences professor. Some participants know one another from years of working in the community on this and other challenges. Beyond the primary purpose of convening to address the homelessness issue, additional benefits for those who will participate include the following:

- Learning more about current program resources of other agencies
- Opportunities to see where organizations, professionals, and researchers have similar interests that match up with agency resources to solve immediate program impediments

Preworkshop Activities for Scenario 4

Step 1: Create a CoLAB team and meet with the United Way director.

In this case, the team will be made up of three public library employees, two of whom have expertise in facilitation and instruction (facilitators) and one with experience coordinating library events. The team schedules a meeting to plan the workshop with the director of the United Way and his program director. The agenda in table 4.6 can help guide the meeting discussion.

Step 2: Prepare the electronic survey that United Way staff will distribute to organization representatives for completion.

See the sidebar for a sample survey.

ELECTRONIC SURVEY FOR ORGANIZATIONS PARTICIPATING IN THE SCENARIO 4 CoLAB WORKSHOP

- Organization:
- Representative name(s):
- E-mail address(es):
- Phone number(s):
- Organization's mission:
- Program names and a brief description of each:
- Number of people served annually by each program:
- Which programs provide HIV/AIDS services?
- Organization's number of staff:
- Number of volunteers:
- Location(s) of facilities:
- Hours of service delivery:
- What do you think are the biggest gaps in information delivery for your homeless patients and clients?
- What do you think are the biggest gaps in information for health care or social service professionals?

A QUICK TIP

When workshop participants are attending as representatives of their organizations, you may want to help them out by sending them an online survey that collects information to prepare the profile-signs prior to the date of the workshop. This can be helpful because organization representatives may find it difficult to recall their organization's profile information without an opportunity to prepare it in advance. In this scenario, library facilitators can already have the signs completed, printed, and ready to go before the workshop begins.

A QUICK TIP

Remember, profile-signs can be customized to reflect different types of assets. For example, while some signs outline the interests and strongest skills of individuals, others can be designed to highlight the mission, goals, and activities of a particular organization.

A QUICK TIP

Usually, when a funding agency is sponsoring a CoLAB, the agency will want to invite groups or individuals with whom they already have long-standing relationships. This is another built-in audience that removes the step of recruitment and guarantees a high level of participation.

TABLE 4.6

AGENDA FOR AN HOUR PLANNING MEETING WITH THE UNITED WAY EXECUTIVE DIRECTOR AND PROGRAM DIRECTOR

TIME	ACTIVITY
10 minutes	Give an overview of a typical CoLAB Workshop, its purpose of connecting strangers with one another's assets, its possible length, and options for workshop agenda activities.
10 minutes	• Confirm the director's desired outcomes to have a community-wide conversation about the barriers to accessing social service and health care information by the homeless population and the possible development of collaborative projects that may result from the workshop. • In this case, the director wants most of the participants to meet one another; the total number of rounds will be twenty-five (25 rounds × 4 minutes = 100 minutes + 45 minutes for editing profile-signs by organization representatives, for preparing profile-signs by the professor and student participants, and for completing the PowerPoint presentation = 145 minutes). Add another sixty-five minutes for the Idea Board activity, group discussion, completing evaluation surveys, and enjoying a light dinner. The grand total of 210 minutes means the session will take three and one-half hours to complete.
35 minutes	Once the length of the workshop has been decided, then through a consensus-building conversation led by the facilitators, develop answers to the following questions: • Other than the facilitators, who will present at the workshop? (Answer: The United Way director will provide brief opening remarks, including an introduction of the CoLAB team, the issues experienced by United Way staff in understanding the barriers to accessing information resources by those who are homeless, and information about the growing number of homeless residents in the community. This will take no more than five minutes.) • How many participants are anticipated and what is the minimum target number to facilitate the workshop? (Answer: For this scenario, a total of forty participant organizations have already agreed to attend. Three organizations want to send two representatives. Five graduate students and their professor also have agreed to attend as a result of United Way's invitation.) • How many conversations is the requester anticipating that the workshop will accommodate? (Answer: The decision is made to anticipate twenty-five rounds of speed-meetings. The workshop will need to be three and one-half hours in length because of United Way staff and space availability.) • What questions will be used on the profile-signs? (Answer: For organization representatives, (1) What is your organization's mission? (2) What programs does your organization provide? (3) How many individuals did your organization serve per program in the past year? (4) Where do you deliver programs? (5) How many staff and how many volunteers serve your organization's clients? Each organization's information will be provided to the facilitators through an electronic survey instrument distributed by United Way staff to their organizations, prior to the workshop, so that profile-signs can be prepared in advance for the workshop. For the professor and his students, (1) What is your current research project as it applies to homelessness issues and why are you passionate about this work? (2) What recent collaborative projects have you been involved in? (3) What are your strengths and skills? (4) What networks or associations or other groups do you participate in? (5) What is one thing most people don't know about you?) • Where will the workshop be presented? (Answer: This workshop will take place in a training room at the United Way facility. The training room is set up classroom style with tables that seat four participants each. It includes a computer, screen, and projector. There is plenty of walking space to accommodate fifty participants as they move from one conversation to another, and if necessary, the tables can be moved to the perimeter of the room during speed-meetings. No room setup is required. The team agrees to visit the training room prior to the workshop to plan for space usage.) • What date and time will the workshop be presented? (Answer: The workshop will be on Thursday, April 12, from 4:30 to 8:00 p.m.) • What will be the title of the workshop? (Answer: The team and United Way directors decide on the title Collaborating on Information Resources for Homeless Clients.) • Does the workshop need to be promoted beyond those being invited to participate by the United Way? (Answer: In Scenario 4, only those organizations and individuals invited by the United Way can attend, and each already has confirmed availability and attendance through individual invitations made by the United Way director.)

TIME	ACTIVITY
35 minutes (continued)	• Who will manage the correspondence with registered participants in preparation for the workshop? (Answer: The CoLAB team will provide the United Way staff with a template for the workshop confirmation e-mail message. An electronic survey will be designed by the facilitators and sent to the United Way for distribution to each participating organization. The survey will include questions for completing the profile-signs so that signs for organizations can be prepopulated, with information gleaned from the surveys, prior to the workshop (see figure 2.8, page 18). A separate e-mail message will be developed by the facilitators for the professor and his five graduate students to confirm their registration and provide them with the profile-sign questions that they will answer upon their arrival at the workshop.) • How will the workshop be evaluated and by whom? (Answer: The United Way program evaluator will design the evaluation instrument and will observe the workshop in person.) • Who will provide dinner? (Answer: The United Way will provide dinner and bottled water.)
5 minutes	Review all of the confirmed decisions and follow-up actions along with the persons responsible for each action to reduce confusion and misunderstandings.

Step 3: Prepare and send an e-mail message with the survey link for organization representatives.

See the sidebar for a sample e-mail.

> ### E-MAIL MESSAGE TO CONFIRM SCENARIO 4 WORKSHOP REGISTRATION FOR ORGANIZATIONS AND TO DISTRIBUTE THE PREWORKSHOP SURVEY LINK
>
> **Subject line:** RE: Registration Survey for Collaborating on Information Resources for Homeless Clients, April 12, 4:30 to 8:00 p.m., United Way Training Room
>
> Thank you for your interest in attending the CoLAB Workshop on Friday, April 12, from 4:30 p.m. to 8:00 p.m., in the training room at United Way. We are asking all of the organization representatives to complete a registration survey (<link>) that will inform activities during the workshop. The deadline for the registration survey is April 5 to confirm your intent to participate.
>
> Dinner will be provided. We look forward to "meeting" you during the workshop!

Step 4: Prepare and send an e-mail message for the professor and his students to confirm their registration.

See the sidebar for a sample e-mail.

E-MAIL MESSAGE TO CONFIRM SCENARIO 4 WORKSHOP REGISTRATION FOR PROFESSOR AND GRADUATE STUDENTS

Subject line: RE: ORIENTATION: Collaborating on Information Resources for Homeless Clients, April 12, 4:30 to 8:00 p.m., United Way Training Room

We're excited that you will be joining us for Collaborating with Strangers to deliver information resources to the homeless. Please read this brief orientation: When you arrive, you will receive a profile-card with the questions listed below. You may prepare answers in advance, if you like. The more detailed the answers to these questions, the more you will benefit from the workshop. But don't worry if you don't have all of the answers—just come and enjoy the experience!

1. What is your current research project as it applies to homelessness issues and why are you passionate about this work?
2. What recent collaborative projects have you been involved in?
3. What are your strengths and skills?
4. What networks or associations or other groups do you participate in?
5. What is one thing most people don't know about you?

Dinner will be provided. If you are interested in learning what past "strangers" had to say about these workshops, check this out: <link>. We look forward to "meeting" you during the workshop!

Step 5: Plan for workshop information to be shared.

In this scenario, the team plans to create a digital flipbook (see Quick Tip, p. 54) that contains images of all the profile-signs along with Idea Board responses and participants' comments related to gaps in information delivery to homeless individuals that were gleaned from the survey.

Step 6: Prepare and print profile-signs for individuals.

For individual participants not representing a community organization, design and print, on 8.5" × 14" legal-size cardstock, blank profile-sign templates and include the five profile questions developed during the planning meeting with the United Way director. Add space for each participant's first name and a box for each participant's

---

A QUICK TIP

In registration forms or confirmation e-mail messages, provide registrants with the opportunity to request assistance due to a disability that necessitates some accommodation during the workshop. Contact information for a campus disability resource center or a human resources office at the sponsoring agency can be included in the registration and confirmation e-mail messages. See chapter 8 for tips on planning for these accommodations.

workshop number, hometown, and home department or area of study. For those who are representing organizations, design a template for featuring the information provided in the survey results. Use the following headings and add boxes for appropriate content: organization name, mission, program names/numbers served (including HIV/AIDS), staff and volunteers (numbers), and facilities (hours of service). For this workshop, a package of Post-it dots for voting will be used. On the back of their profile-signs, participants will find space for providing the workshop date along with their names and e-mail addresses and brief instructions about the major workshop steps: preparing profile-signs, completing permissions, participating in speed-meetings, and completing the postworkshop survey.

Step 7: Prepare and print profile-signs for organization representatives.

For organization representatives, design and print information gleaned from the pre-workshop survey results on two 8.5" × 14" legal-size sheets of paper, using the landscape format. Affix these sheets to card stock 19" high × 16" wide to make the front of the organization profile-signs. (See an example of this type of profile-sign in figure 2.10, page 20.) Print the one-page postworkshop evaluation surveys and permission forms, and affix them to the back of the organization profile-signs.

Step 8: Organize supplies.

Other supplies include a blank checklist with space for writing participant numbers and correlating notes or reminders about ideas from speed-meeting conversations, name tags to be used for participant numbers (not their names), Sharpie fine-point markers, flipchart paper, 3" × 3" Post-it notes, and safety pins.

Step 9: Create and confirm the workshop agenda.

Create a workshop agenda, including time calculations, similar to the one in table 4.7.

Step 10: Plan CoLAB team roles.

Do this in the same manner as described in Scenario 1, Step 9 (see page 54).

Day-of-Workshop Activities for Scenario 4

In this scenario, the workshop begins at 4:30 p.m. and ends at 8:00 p.m.

TABLE 4.7

AGENDA FOR COLLABORATING WITH STRANGERS TO DELIVER INFORMATION RESOURCES TO THE HOMELESS CoLAB WORKSHOP

TIME	ACTIVITY
4:15 to 4:45	Participants arrive and each receives a profile-sign, fine-point Sharpie marker, and workshop number label.
4:45 to 5:05	• Participants arriving late continue to complete the previous steps. • The United Way director introduces facilitators and provides an overview of issues facing community providers of services related to connecting homeless clients with information resources. • A member of the CoLAB team gives a PowerPoint presentation. [The detailed contents of the presentation were described previously in this chapter, beginning on page 59.]
5:05 to 6:05	• Participants are instructed to raise their right hands and repeat the facilitator's instruction: "I promise to move when I hear the bell." The facilitator explains why moving to a new participant is so important to keeping the process moving and organized. • Participants are instructed to stay seated or stand, whichever is more comfortable. • The speed-meeting process begins with everyone finding a partner. In the case where there are an odd number of participants, a speed-meeting pairing will include three participants instead of two.
6:05 to 6:35	• Facilitate the speed-meeting process. • Participants are instructed that the final speed-meeting conversation has occurred and to take a seat. • Dinner is served.
6:35 to 6:45	Facilitators post three flipchart sheets–Idea Boards–on the training room wall with these three headings: (1) What synergies did you discover? (2) What things did you learn? (3) What are your next steps? Each participant is given a stack of ten 3" × 3" Post-it notes. Participants are instructed to write as many answers to the questions as possible, one answer per Post-it. They are asked to place their Post-it notes on the appropriate Idea Board.
6:45 to 7:20	Use poster-size printouts of the survey answers (affixed to the wall or foam core) for these questions: (1) What do you think are the biggest gaps in information delivery for your homeless patients and clients? (2) What do you think are the biggest gaps in information for health care or social service professionals? A facilitator instructs participants to review the survey answers and to add additional responses to these lists of answers by writing them directly on the printouts. Participants receive six Post-it dots for voting on the three most significant responses to each question. A facilitator leads an open discussion about results and next steps.
7:20 to 7:30	Participants are instructed to complete their permission forms and evaluation surveys and to return their markers, profile-signs, and evaluations. A facilitator shares information about the follow-up e-mail message that all participants will receive, which will include a link to view the profile-signs, contact information, Idea Board responses, and responses/votes related to the two survey questions.

FIGURE 4.21

FLOWCHART FOR SCENARIO 4–PREWORKSHOP ACTIVITIES

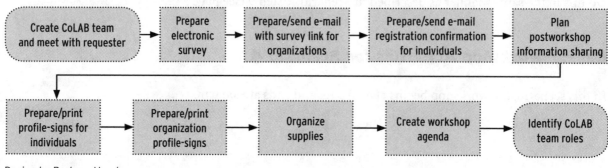

Design by Barbara Hood

FIGURE 4.22

FLOOR PLAN FOR SCENARIO 4—PUBLIC LIBRARY

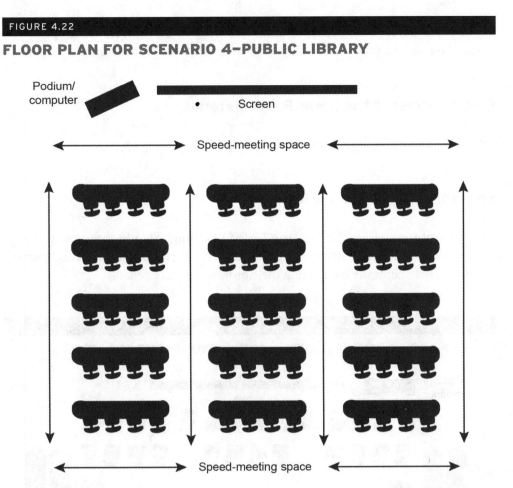

Design by Barbara Hood

Step 11: Dispense instructions and supplies to participants.

As individual participants arrive, regardless of how early, they will want to get started preparing their profile-sign information (in the case of the students and professor) using the Sharpie fine-point marker. Participants who are representing organizations are provided with their profile-signs, which include responses to survey questions related to each organization's assets. Instruct organization representatives to review their profile-signs for accuracy and completeness and to make corrections and additions using a Sharpie marker. When two participants represent the same organization, only one profile-sign is needed.

Step 12: Have participants edit information on their prepopulated organization profile-signs, and have the professor and his students complete their individual profile-signs.

Organization representatives review the content of their profile-signs for any inaccuracies or for information that was excluded. They correct text and add information that

A QUICK TIP

In a workshop with community organizations, headshots are not necessary. Participants are more focused on the identity of the organization rather than on the appearance of the representatives.

will be important for CoLAB participants to learn, using the Sharpie markers provided. Allow about ten minutes for individuals to complete their profile-signs.

Step 13: Present the PowerPoint material.

Follow the process outlined in Scenario 1, Step 13 (beginning on page 59).

Step 14: Conduct the workshop.

Follow the process outlined in Scenario 1, Step 14 through Step 18 (beginning on page 61). Even if not all of the participants have arrived, begin the presentation and encourage everyone to continue completing their profile-signs as needed.

FIGURE 4.23

ALTERNATE FLOOR PLAN FOR SCENARIO 4—PUBLIC LIBRARY

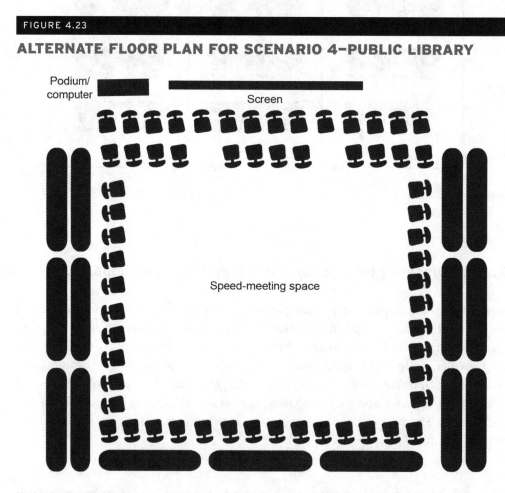

Design by Barbara Hood

Step 19: Debrief survey responses to the two questions about providing information resources to homeless residents.

Check in to determine if participants need a ten-minute break before debriefing. To debrief, use poster-size printouts of the survey answers (affixed to the wall or foam core) for these questions: (1) What do you think are the biggest gaps in information delivery for your homeless patients and clients? (2) What do you think are the biggest gaps in information for health care or social service professionals? A facilitator instructs participants to review the survey answers and to add additional responses related to these questions by writing them directly on the printouts using the Sharpie markers.

Step 20: Initiate voting on the survey responses.

The team distributes six Post-it dots to each participant. After reviewing all of the answers provided, participants are directed to choose which three answers related to each question will receive their endorsement (one Post-it dot) as the most accurate and significant answers. Participants place dots on the printouts to represent their votes.

Step 21: Debrief the outcomes of the voting process.

A facilitator leads a debriefing discussion by first determining which answers to the first question received the most votes. To allow for more discussion, the facilitator poses additional questions that help reveal participants' views about possible causes for the gaps that received the most votes. Repeat the process for the second question. A team member takes notes during the discussion. The facilitator summarizes the discussion and indicates that the workshop has arrived at its conclusion.

Step 22: Have participants complete permissions forms and evaluation surveys and encourage them to follow-up after the workshop.

Instruct participants to complete their evaluation surveys, contact information, and the permissions form (for sharing photographs). Provide information about the follow-up e-mail message that will include a link to the profile-signs, contact information, transcripts of the Idea Board responses, photographs taken during the speed-meeting process, and a list of answers to the two questions along with concluding notes summarizing the discussion.

A QUICK TIP

CoLAB Workshops also can bring together individuals as well as organizations. This is a great approach for a student organization or study abroad or volunteer fair where groups are looking to meet and recruit new members.

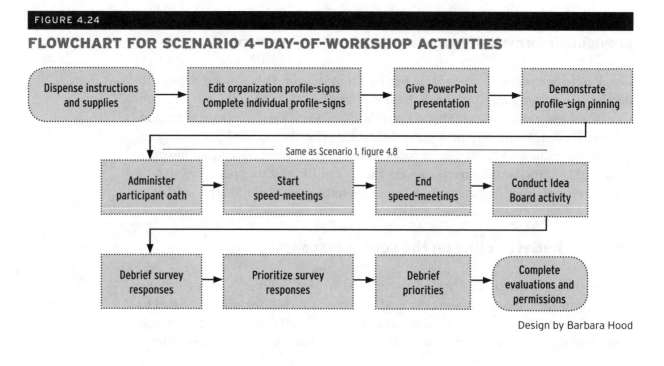

FIGURE 4.24

FLOWCHART FOR SCENARIO 4—DAY-OF-WORKSHOP ACTIVITIES

Dispense instructions and supplies → Edit organization profile-signs / Complete individual profile-signs → Give PowerPoint presentation → Demonstrate profile-sign pinning

Same as Scenario 1, figure 4.8

Administer participant oath → Start speed-meetings → End speed-meetings → Conduct Idea Board activity

Debrief survey responses → Prioritize survey responses → Debrief priorities → Complete evaluations and permissions

Design by Barbara Hood

Postworkshop Activities for Scenario 4

Step 23: Verify evaluation surveys and permission forms.

For this scenario, also review the content for organization profile-signs to see if edits have been made to correct or add new information about each organization. Make sure that these changes are made to the electronic versions of the profile-signs in preparation for sharing them with participants.

Step 24: Process the profile-signs.

Scan profile-signs in alphabetical order according to organization name, including profiles of the professor and students using the name of the university, into one large PDF.

Step 25: Transcribe the responses provided on the three Idea Boards and the comments made in response to the two survey questions.

Special attention should be given to this task to ensure that a complete record of the CoLAB Workshop outputs can be shared with all participants. This is important because organization representatives may want to share these proceedings with their organization colleagues.

E-MAIL MESSAGE TO SHARE SCENARIO 4 POST-CoLAB WORKSHOP INFORMATION

Subject line: CoLAB Workshop Follow-Up Information

Dear United Way Director,
Thank you for hosting the CoLAB Workshop Collaborating with Strangers to Deliver Information Resources to the Homeless. The CoLAB team has organized information from participants who agreed to share their profiles as well as the Idea Board responses and answers to the survey questions and discussion. The resulting PDF is attached. If this meets with your approval, please forward this message to the organization representatives, professor, and students at your earliest convenience, or let us know if you have recommendations for modifying the attachment.

The CoLAB team appreciates all of the resources you and your United Way staff contributed to making the workshop a success.

Step 26: Share workshop materials.

Create a digital flipbook or one comprehensive PDF for sharing workshop profiles, Idea Board responses, and answers to the two survey questions including voting results.

Step 27: Prepare and send a postworkshop e-mail message to the United Way for review and distribution to participants.

See the sidebar for a sample message.

Step 28: Analyze evaluation surveys and prepare an evaluation report.

In this scenario, the analysis of evaluation surveys, compilation of observations, and production of the report will be the role of the United Way program evaluator. The report should be sent to the CoLAB team to ensure accuracy of the information.

Step 29: Share the evaluation report with the United Way director.

Suggest that the evaluation report be distributed to workshop participants at the director's discretion.

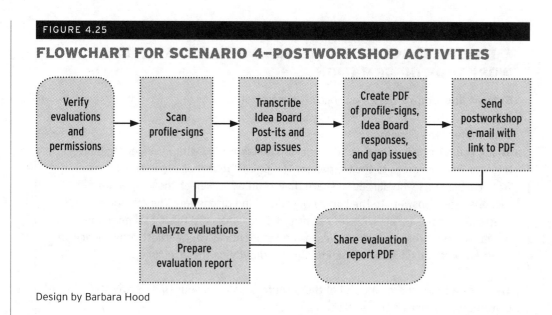

FIGURE 4.25

FLOWCHART FOR SCENARIO 4–POSTWORKSHOP ACTIVITIES

Design by Barbara Hood

Variations on CoLAB Workshop Activities

There are many ways to facilitate the development of new collaborative relationships beyond the four scenarios described in chapter 4. This chapter provides brief examples focused on achieving a variety of purposes and also for serving different types of participants. These descriptions present actual workshops that have been facilitated by the authors in recent years and share options for profile-signs, participant checklists, and hands-on activities that together support collaboration development.

Icebreakers

Modifying a CoLAB Workshop for an icebreaker activity that takes from ten minutes up to thirty minutes can transform a room of strangers into a comfortable environment. This method has been used at the start of several training workshops, such as collaborative grant-seeking basics and introduction to facilitation techniques for graduate students. It also has facilitated connections during student organization meetings focused on enhancing research collaborations or getting to know new members. (See figure 5.1.)

FIGURE 5.1

CoLAB ICEBREAKER DURING THE FLORIDA LIBRARY ASSOCIATION ANNUAL CONFERENCE

Photo by Bess de Farber

Provide each participant with an index card. Instruct participants to answer a question that can be preprinted on the card with a label or written on a PowerPoint slide for everyone to view. Give participants about five minutes to answer the question using a pen so that the answers will be easily readable. (See figure 5.2.) Then instruct them to find a partner whom they don't know and to read each other's cards. The partners then have a conversation that can be related to what was written on either card or to any other topic they might choose to discuss. One three- to four-minute conversation may be all the time you have, but this activity can be repeated over several rounds so that each participant can engage with four to five strangers. The goal is to quickly create a sense of intimacy in the room. Some underlying objectives that may be achieved during the icebreaker could include exposing hidden assets, providing means for sharing resources or referrals, or simply finding a partner with whom to share time during the workshop lunch. People are often surprised at how much they have in common, how interested they are in others' pursuits that are completely different from their own, or how much they can learn in a very short time frame.

FIGURE 5.2

EXAMPLE OF ICEBREAKER PROMPT AND PARTICIPANT ANSWER DURING FLORIDA LIBRARY ASSOCIATION ANNUAL CONFERENCE

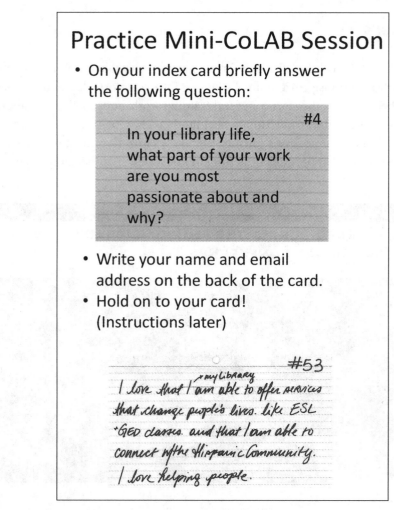

Practice Mini-CoLAB Session

- On your index card briefly answer the following question:

  #4
  In your library life, what part of your work are you most passionate about and why?

- Write your name and email address on the back of the card.
- Hold on to your card! (Instructions later)

#53
I love that I am able to offer services ^my library
that change people's lives. like ESL
+GED classes. and that I am able to
connect w/the Hispanic Community.
I love helping people.

Conference Sessions

Conferences are perfect venues to facilitate elements of a CoLAB Workshop, whether as a plenary session for a large group or as an individual conference session for a group interested in a more specific topic. Conference CoLAB Workshops work well because of the homogeneity of participants who have self-selected to join other like-minded people or those with similar career types. More so than convening a CoLAB Workshop in an academic environment that doesn't have a theme, participants at a conference already come to a destination with a predetermined theme.

Elements of CoLAB Workshops have been presented, for instance, at the Association of College & Research Libraries (ACRL) as a preconference workshop with sixty-three participants; as a plenary session at the Living the Future 7: Transforming Libraries through Collaboration conference with 120 participants; as a session within the ACRL Scholarly Communication 101 Road Show; and as a conference presentation at the Florida Library Association Annual Conference. In each instance, the session brought together people who were at the conference to meet, learn from, and work with strangers for the first time, to efficiently communicate their own individual and institutional assets and interests, and to make new discoveries about people, places, methodologies, and opportunities, to name a few outcomes. CoLABs at conferences create opportunities for quick, intimate conversations that can enhance the overall conference experience and open attendees to the possibilities that result from deliberately meeting new people. The number of meaningful connections made during a CoLAB experience can far exceed the average number achieved using traditional networking techniques. (See figure 5.3.)

FIGURE 5.3

CoLAB SPEED-MEETINGS AT ASSOCIATION OF COLLEGE & RESEARCH LIBRARIES ANNUAL CONFERENCE

Photo by Bess de Farber

Presenting a CoLAB session at a conference requires lots of planning, especially if facilitators need to travel by air to reach the conference venue, which can limit transport of necessary supplies. Planning the methodology for facilitating a CoLAB session always hinges on the amount of time available and access to the necessary supplies. Here are some options:

- Bring three different-colored 7" × 5" index cards, with one color assigned to each question so participants don't need to rewrite the question. With tape, a safety pin, and a Sharpie marker, each participant can create his or her own profile-sign by taping the cards together horizontally and punching a hole at the top of the first question card.
- Preprint, on 8.5" × 14" card stock, and hole-punch a profile-sign template, as described in chapter 4, that includes five questions that typically appear on Collaborating with Strangers profile-signs.
- Use blank 8.5" × 14" card stock and affix three to five sheets of Post-it–lined paper, size 6" × 4", to the blank card stock (see figure 5.3). Each sheet can provide space to answer a question that appears on a PowerPoint slide.

Once participants have created their signs at the start of the workshop, the presenter can review the purpose of the workshop, share some or all of the standard PowerPoint presentation described in chapter 4, and complete a CoLAB session using timed speed-meeting rounds of conversations, a checklist for capturing notes about conversations, and Idea Boards for debriefing the session, if time allows. Another debriefing method is to have everyone sit in groups at Idea Tables, as described in chapter 3, where they can list all of the possible connections made along with identified new projects or resources on which to follow up. Instruct participants to spend a few minutes sharing some examples of these connections so others can benefit from the possibilities that emerged during the session. In this scenario, it is critical to provide contact information and each person's corresponding workshop participant number so that attendees can follow up with one another after the session when they have returned home.

Classroom Settings

CoLAB sessions facilitated during a class can change the dynamics of class interaction. These have been used on the first day of a class or early in the course simply to introduce students to one another. They have been so successful that for the past several years, CoLABs have been requested by instructors teaching an Introduction to Research course for first-year undergraduate honors students and a Grant Writing course for graduate students pursuing any discipline, both at the University of Florida. The method also was used with much success to create new business teams at the University of Arizona in the McGuire Center Entrepreneurship Program. During classes, the goal should be that all students have sufficient time to meet one another, which may take two classroom sessions to complete, using a three- to five-question format.

In higher education environments, and especially in large institutions, many students may never have the opportunity or the courage to meet and get to know the other students who will be sitting near them every day for an entire semester. CoLAB Workshops offer an efficient means for eliminating the discomfort of talking to strangers in classrooms and allow students to practice the art of conversation. As in the conference setting, there is no need to create a theme, but a theme can be added within the questions to reveal the types of assets that would be most beneficial during the CoLAB vis-à-vis the topic of the course or class. (See figure 5.4.)

FIGURE 5.4

SPEED-MEETING DURING A CoLAB FOR PUBLIC RELATIONS STUDENTS

Photo by Barbara Hood

Nonprofit Organization Representatives Working in a Common Geographical Area

CoLAB Workshops have been very popular with nonprofit organization boards and staff members. This may be because leveraging one another's assets in this sector has been valued for decades. The roots of community development and the organizing of individuals around a cause for which to advocate, raise money, or provide services—including academic pursuits—has been part of the American philanthropic culture since the establishment of Harvard University, the first nonprofit organization in the United States. A nonprofit organization's contacts and relationships are its bread and butter.

CoLAB Workshops for nonprofit participants, in the best-case scenario, should be sponsored and convened by a community funding agency. These types of workshops have been presented or sponsored by such organizations as United Way agencies, Community Foundations, a Junior League, a Children's Services Council, a division of a health department, and a local arts agency. Historically in this scenario, individual participants have not paid to attend these workshops. Rather, all expenses have been covered by the sponsor or presenting agency. This sponsorship format could be altered, of course, to suit any other circumstance.

The beauty of not imposing a theme on these CoLAB Workshops is that the common geographic area in which all participating representatives work and serve becomes the theme, while at the same time encouraging the cross-pollination of organizations in different disciplines. For instance, the Sonoran Desert CoLAB held at the University of Arizona Library in Tucson attracted representatives from twenty-seven organizations from throughout the communities surrounding this desert as well as several based in Phoenix that were working in this area. This CoLAB served to convene those based in a geographical area, which also served as an overarching theme. Participants represented museums, botanical and bird-related organizations, educational centers, environmental protection groups, libraries, and research institutes on multiple topics, among other organization types. (See figure 5.5.)

FIGURE 5.5

CoLAB FOR NONPROFIT ORGANIZATIONS AND GOVERNMENT AGENCIES WORKING IN THE SONORAN DESERT

Photo by Bess de Farber

Preparing profile-signs in advance allows participants sufficient time to meet representatives of all the organizations attending the workshop. Facilitators should use a survey method, accompanied by follow-up phone calls with those registered to attend, to access sufficient information about an organization's mission, programs, facilities, number of clients served by the program in a given year, hours of operation, types of clients serviced, partnerships with other nonprofit or government organizations, and any other similar information. This process can take quite a while depending on the number of organizations represented, which should not be more than fifty per workshop. (See figure 5.6.)

FIGURE 5.6

COMPLETED PROFILE-SIGNS LINING THE WALL PRIOR TO NONPROFIT ORGANIZATION SPEED-MEETINGS

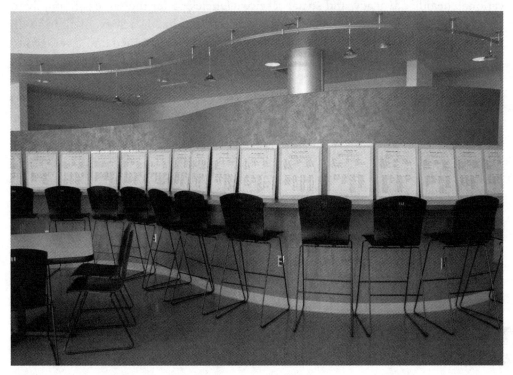

Photo by Bess de Farber

When you have this many people in a CoLAB session, it may be best to organize the profiles-signs in alphabetical order by organization name, as was done for the Belle Glade CoLAB described in chapter 2. Prior to the CoLAB Workshop, divide the list in half or in quarters to form separate groups that each can be assigned a color. This allows for a more structured facilitated environment where it is easier to find a partner. Let's say that you have two groups, each with twenty-five representatives. In this case, for the first speed-meetings, invite the green signs to meet one another and the yellow signs to meet one another. When this activity has been completed, take a break. Then have the green signs meet the yellow signs after the break. These workshops typically take at least six hours and can run as long as one and a half days or several partial days.

Much can be achieved with nonprofit organization representatives who attend CoLAB Workshops. Most have had experience in combining forces with other organizations, whether in cooperative, coordinative, collaborative, or mentoring arrangements. Participants often have had experiences in facilitated workshops that encourage one-on-one or small-group conversations for strategic or event planning. But there are always new staff and board members, new programs or facilities, mergers and partnerships, or other types of transformations happening in this sector, so there is plenty to learn during a CoLAB Workshop even if participants claim they "know" one another. Because the partners can be very diverse in their expertise and missions, these workshops are often convened with the intent of creating a plan or plans for solving community issues in creative and unexpected ways.

"When I signed up I only expected the possibility of collaborating with groups based in our city, only one . . . but ended up with 8 great opportunities from organizations all over the county. Very exciting and informative—time flew by!"

—CoLAB Workshop participant representing the City of Boynton Beach*

*April Hines, "Comments Made by Participants after Attending a CoLAB Workshop 2002-2016" (PDF document, 2016), http://ufdc.ufl.edu/IR00008472/00001, 1.

CoLAB Workshops already have helped hundreds of nonprofit groups and government agencies connect to other organizations in new ways and in new configurations across disciplinary boundaries. Combining cultural, scientific, environmental, educational, health, advocacy, and social service agencies under the same roof purely to learn about one another's assets can be considered a valuable achievement in itself. Imagining the possibilities of how these assets can be recombined and leveraged to improve services while increasing the numbers of individuals served is a powerful prospect by any measure.

Beyond the opening presentation and the speed-meeting process, other activities during the session can broaden a workshop's objectives. For example, after all participants have met one another, consider adding an activity that allows small groups of five to ten people (depending on total attendance) to produce an object together. This could be the production of a zine (see figure 5.7), a found public art object, a campaign slogan or logo, or the tallest freestanding newspaper tower. Designate one person in each group to serve as a neutral observer who will share his or her observations and feedback during the activity debriefing. The observer also can impart recommendations for improving the team's effectiveness. Instruct the groups (which should be engaged in the same activity) about their time limit and their ultimate goal. Groups can vote on the best product or choose an independent group of participants to select the best-performing team.

FIGURE 5.7

EXAMPLE OF ZINE PRODUCED BY PARTICIPANTS DURING A CoLAB WORKSHOP

Another activity that can provide learning and planning results for organization representatives after the speed-meetings is to have organizations self-identify as to whether they are primarily providers or primarily receivers of services. There are basically three types of nonprofit organizations represented at CoLAB Workshops: (1) service providers, those which develop programs or projects to serve audiences and clients outside of their organizations (such as a literacy coalition); (2) service receivers, those which execute programs or projects to serve their internal or recurring audiences and clients (such as a day care center); and (3) those which do a little bit of both (such as a homeless shelter). In contrast to these three categories of nonprofits, advocacy organizations, whose mission is primarily advocacy of an issue or advocacy for changing governmental policies, have historically made up only a small minority of the organizations represented at CoLAB Workshops.

For the activity described here, begin by selecting five or six service providers, each of which will be featured in small-group discussions. Each provider organization is given a flipchart and easel where a scribe will capture notes (this could be the selected representative of each featured organization). Participants form small groups around each easel. They are instructed by facilitators to restrict the small-group discussion to posing questions about the featured organization's services, such as how to access different services, the cost of services, the length of time for completing the service delivery, and other inquiries to clarify these organizations' assets. After approximately twenty minutes, a new set of five or six service provider organizations are featured while the participants switch to a second or third group for a new round of inquiries. Answers to these questions are not disseminated during the workshop. Instead, as a follow-up to the workshop, all of the questions related to each of these provider organizations that have been recorded on the easel pads will be answered by the organization representatives and then distributed to all participants by the facilitators. This is an excellent way to expedite the planning process for forming partnerships with organizations that were represented in the workshop.

Finally, the facilitators may want to address the issues of organizational needs within the context of a CoLAB Workshop. To prepare for this activity, the team must develop a method for capturing the needs of the organizations planning to attend the CoLAB. This can be achieved by including a question in the registration survey that asks, "Beyond funding, what are your organization's needs in order of priority (this can include client needs)?" Or, following the speed-meeting process at the workshop, the facilitator can ask participants to post a sheet of their organizations' needs on the easel papers distributed on the walls throughout the room. Using either method to collect the lists of needs, spend about thirty minutes, depending on the number of organizations, to allow participants to review these lists and to use 3" × 3" Post-its to share ideas for how some of the organizations might meet or contribute to reducing these needs. Suggestions can include referrals to resources outside or within the organizations represented at the workshop.

The needs lists may reveal that a number of organizations have similar needs, such as backpacks for school-aged youth. Simply revealing this one common need could be the start of a coordinated effort to seek and distribute backpacks provided by a common sponsor to a variety of locations in a single county. This proposal may be perfect for an in-kind corporate sponsorship provided by Office Depot.

PARTICIPANT QUOTE

"I think it was very interesting and useful. It helps 'break down' the barriers that some may have regarding networking and pooling resources, and openly discussing your fundraising techniques, budgets, and board development. Even recognizing that you have resources and discovering them."

–**Participant in the Broward County CoLAB Planning Series Workshop***

*April Hines, "Comments Made by Participants after Attending a CoLAB Workshop 2002-2016" (PDF document, 2016), http://ufdc.ufl.edu/IR00008472/00001, 1.

PARTICIPANT QUOTE

"Fabulous networking opportunity. . . . This was an incredibly productive workshop. . . . Problems/ difficulties of area services, etc. . . . Connectivity and awareness of other organizations/resources. . . . Understanding of needs . . ."

–**Participant in the Palm Beach County CoLAB Planning Series Workshop***

*April Hines, "Comments Made by Participants after Attending a CoLAB Workshop 2002-2016" (PDF document, 2016), http://ufdc.ufl.edu/IR00008472/00001, 2.

"Meeting other organizational representatives. Learning more about those I already knew, and meeting new individuals and learning about their organizations. I think everything was useful. I would recommend it to those who have no previous collaborative experience."

—**Participant at HIV/AIDS Prevention in Youth***

*April Hines, "Comments Made by Participants after Attending a CoLAB Workshop 2002-2016" (PDF document, 2016), http://ufdc.ufl.edu/IR00008472/00001, 1.

"Meeting different kinds of people allowed for different perspectives on how people [felt about] sustainability. Also having faculty/student interaction is interesting."

—**Participant at Collaborating with Strangers on Sustainability Projects***

*April Hines, "Comments Made by Participants after Attending a CoLAB Workshop 2002-2016" (PDF document, 2016), http://ufdc.ufl.edu/IR00008472/00001, 1.

Topic-Based Sessions

Any CoLAB can be converted into one that is topic based. For instance, CoLAB Workshops have featured the following themes:

- Sustainability
- Grant Seeking
- HIV/AIDS Information Gaps
- Books and Objects of Study
- County Literacy Gaps
- Sex and Gender Differences in Health
- The Sonoran Desert
- Food Research
- GIS (Geographic Information Systems) Day
- Digital Scholarship
- Dissertation Boot Camp
- Librarian In-Service
- Communications and Health

During these types of workshops, the CoLAB team can decide to add a planning component to the workshop that supports participants in brainstorming answers to questions that can then be prioritized and used for future decision-making and planning actions. For example, a CoLAB Workshop sponsored by the United Way in Martin County, Florida, convened thirty-five organizations that were all being impacted by literacy deficiencies among populations in the county, including school-aged children, prisoners, low-wage service workers, immigrant families, and other groups. Participants were organized into groups to elicit perspectives regarding the various causes of literacy gaps in these populations. After all of the groups had completed and debriefed their answers, participants voted on those causes for which solutions could rapidly be deployed. (See figure 5.8.)

Grant Proposal Development Incentives

For sponsors seeking to solve a community problem through a grant-making program, presenting a CoLAB Workshop on the topic can be an effective means for incentivizing new innovative collaborative partnerships. Executives at the United Way of Palm Beach County, Florida, were seeking to fund projects to increase HIV/AIDS prevention in youth. One of its donors was interested in reducing the incidence of infection in the county's youth, which had become a growing problem. A series of three, three-hour CoLAB Workshops, which included invited nonprofit providers and youth in middle and high schools, was presented over a three-week period. The workshops included (1) speed-meetings to allow for conversations with organizations and students who learned about one another's assets and interests, (2) small-group brainstorming and discussion of all the ways in which youth have access to information and health care screenings, (3) presentations by the youth participants, who shared information on how they learn

FIGURE 5.8

SPEED-MEETINGS DURING A CoLAB ON COMMUNICATION TOPICS

Photo by Barbara Hood

about health care and HIV/AIDS prevention methods, and (4) prioritizing methods for removing the barriers to learning about these diseases, prevention methods, and access to testing. Lastly, participants self-selected others in the workshop with whom to establish partnerships and to prepare grant proposals for review by United Way staff. One of the many results from this CoLAB was the funding of a new partnership between Catholic Charities and the American Red Cross to increase awareness of HIV/AIDS among young immigrants from Guatemala who were living in central Palm Beach County. (See figure 5.9.)

FIGURE 5.9

SPEED-MEETINGS DURING A CoLAB ON HIV/AIDS PREVENTION IN YOUTH

Photo by Bess de Farber

PARTICIPANT QUOTE

"The CoLAB helped me connect others with resources/contacts. I don't do research; I facilitate it!"

–UF staff member at CoLAB Workshop for those interested in applying for grant funding*

*April Hines, "Comments Made by Participants after Attending a CoLAB Workshop 2002-2016" (PDF document, 2016), http://ufdc.ufl.edu/IR00008472/00001, 1.

Matchmaking for Dissimilar Disciplinary Groups or Participants with Different Types of Expertise

When members of two or more different types of groups or organizations want to increase their potential for forming partnerships, CoLAB Workshops can be used to accomplish this end. For example, members of the Women in Science and Engineering (WiSE) organization at the University of Florida sought to increase the number of female faculty mentors to be paired up with their student members. They requested a CoLAB Workshop intended to attract fifteen engineering and science faculty and fifteen WiSE organization members. In this case, the best scenario is to have equal representation from each group and to distinguish the groups by using a different color for the profile-signs for each group or simply by adding a colored ribbon to each profile-sign, thereby helping participants to find the faculty or the student participants quickly. (See figure 5.10.)

FIGURE 5.10

SPEED-MEETINGS DURING A CoLAB FOR WOMEN IN SCIENCE AND ENGINEERING FACULTY AND STUDENTS

Photo by Barbara Hood

Faculty members themselves often work in silos, whether they intend to do so or whether it is simply a byproduct of limited available time. Two examples illustrate the power of bringing together groups of faculty members working in different disciplines. First, during a day-long faculty orientation for the College of Arts at the University of Florida, over 100 faculty from theatre, dance, art and art history, and music convened for a CoLAB speed-meeting process (rather than a complete workshop). (See figure 5.11.)

By using different-colored signs to represent the four departments, faculty were instructed not to partner with anyone with whom they had worked in the past or with anyone from their own departments. Each participant conversed with eleven strangers, sharing their current projects and rationale for pursuing arts instruction as their careers.

Another example was combining faculty from the College of Journalism and Communications, and the College of Public Health and Health Professions at the University of Florida. This again focused on individual research projects and initiating discussions about ways in which faculty could join forces on existing or proposed future projects.

FIGURE 5.11

SPEED-MEETINGS DURING A CoLAB FOR FACULTY FROM DIFFERENT DEPARTMENTS IN THE SAME COLLEGE

Photo by Barbara Hood

Seeking Sponsors for CoLAB Workshops

CoLAB Workshops create excellent opportunities for acquiring public and private sponsorship. This chapter outlines strategies, along with sample excerpts from proposals, for requesting sponsorship support. These practical steps reflect some of the successful strategies that have supported the facilitation, promotion, and postworkshop activities previously described in chapters 2 and 5.

Step 1: Determine What Type of Support Is Needed

Your CoLAB team should answer a couple questions to start the process. First, is the team planning to facilitate one workshop or a series of four to six workshops? Knowing the answer to this question will determine the type of resources that will be necessary. For instance, if you plan to facilitate only one community workshop, then many of the team's existing resources may be sufficient to complete it successfully. If your team plans to present a series of four to six workshops, then this may require additional support. Regardless, the next question should be this: What resources or assets already are available for presenting and facilitating a CoLAB Workshop? Here is a list of what would be necessary to facilitate either one workshop or a series of workshops—assuming that facilitators will be volunteering their time:

- Graphic design expertise for creating the profile-sign templates and promotional materials and cropping the participant headshots
- Printing for the profile-sign templates and promotional materials
- Scanning services for the completed profile-signs
- Communication with registrants and participants
- Refreshments or a meal depending on the design and length of the workshop(s)
- Supplies, including Sharpie markers, lanyards, Post-its, and pens
- Website, blog, or Facebook development and maintenance to have a constant CoLAB Workshop presence; to retain publicity, comments, and Idea Board results; and to encourage participants to browse profiles of "strangers" they met during past workshops
- Evaluation services, either in-house or external, including the design, analysis, and creation of reports for translating the qualitative and quantitative

IN THIS CHAPTER

✓ Step 1: Determine What Type of Support Is Needed

✓ Step 2: Search for a Sponsor

✓ Step 3: Prepare a Grant or Sponsorship Proposal

✓ Step 4: Add CoLAB Workshops to Enhance Other Proposed Grant Projects

✓ Notes

workshop results to fuel future workshop interest and support, satisfy sponsor requirements, and provide inspiration for the CoLAB team

- An adequate space to accommodate the number of anticipated participants, the type of activities, and the refreshments or meals planned in the workshop agenda

With this list in mind, the team should determine what assets it lacks to successfully present its workshop or series of workshops. Sufficient lead time should be available to do the following:

- Search for possible sponsors
- Determine the feasibility of applying to selected sponsors
- Prepare the sponsorship letter of inquiry, the sponsorship package (for corporations), or a grant application, as required

Step 2: Search for a Sponsor

With these answers, the CoLAB team is ready to search for a sponsor. If the workshop or series of workshops will be thematic to contribute toward resolving a community issue or supporting a community cause, then considering a request to a local sponsor may be the best option. This can be achieved through the submission of a formal grant proposal, if this is required, or through a letter of inquiry to a sponsor whose mission matches the theme of the workshop. Consider the following two scenarios.

Scenario 1

In this scenario, the CoLAB team's goal is to link together organizations that are all working on community environmental and sustainability issues. In searching the local Community Foundation's key funding interests, the team learns that funding is available for proposals that support environmental improvement programs. A proposal is developed in collaboration with the local high school to present a series of CoLAB Workshops on the theme of sustainability. The CoLAB team gains a partnership through the local college, whose students are engaged in environmental studies. To prove the efficacy of the CoLAB Workshop for inspiring new collaborative partnerships and projects, the expanded team requests $5,000 to cover refreshments, lunch, and postworkshop evaluation services for a series of four workshops. The CoLAB team determines that with the help of students, all of the design and online presence requirements will be contributed. To identify an external evaluator, the team decides to contact the academic institution within the local community. The evaluator can be a graduate student or faculty member in the social sciences or a discipline related to the workshop theme. The third-party evaluator's role may be tracking the progress of partnerships that were inspired during the CoLAB Workshop and developed over the following three to six months.

Scenario 2

In this scenario, the CoLAB team members all work for an academic library and want to adapt these workshops to offer an ongoing library collaboration program. They plan to create an interactive website to facilitate online follow-up with workshop participants but lack available IT personnel for website development and maintenance. The CoLAB team also lacks available staff to directly promote the workshops among the student body. The team seeks to present a series of workshops on campus without imposing a theme, but rather promoting the concept of multidisciplinary research and delivering structured and comfortable environments in which to inspire these types of partnerships, whether collaborative, coordinative, cooperative, or mentoring in nature.

The library has an endowment fund that is used primarily to support innovative projects. Another funding source may be a campus sponsorship program that annually provides support for projects that produce diverse research teams or other types of innovative projects. A proposal for $5,000 may be sufficient to hire a student at twelve hours per week for one or two semesters to handle the promotion of the four workshops, the initial design and postworkshop processing of materials, and the updating of the website following each workshop. To cover the need for an external evaluator, the team invites a graduate student from the College of Education to evaluate workshop benefits and results, including interviewing student participants to learn about how the workshops impacted their outlook on connecting with strangers and any results that occurred as a result of participating in the workshop. The benefits of having the graduate student's analysis published on the CoLAB Workshop website, in the library's open access repository, and in a journal article that the CoLAB team plans to submit for publication are attractive incentives for securing a qualified graduate student evaluator.

Increasingly, sponsors are looking to invest in opportunities that further collaboration and promote innovation. These themes have become ubiquitous in the philanthropic sector. To benefit from this trend, those wanting to present CoLAB Workshops should consider forming a sponsorship team of interested library staff and librarians. The goal of the team may be to search for and capture information that identifies which sponsors locally, regionally, and nationally are interested in supporting the themes of collaboration and innovation development within educational or nonprofit settings. Here is some advice to keep in mind when searching for funding:

Searching for library funding can be challenging. Beyond discerning the type of funding being granted, or the type of agency that is administering the grant-making process, librarians who are searching for viable funding options can miss opportunities for other reasons. For instance, searching for sponsors that support libraries may be a good place to start, but this method has several limitations. Search results often yield funding information that is restricted to libraries located in a specific region of the country. The trick is in knowing that it is not necessarily about whether or not a sponsor funds libraries. It is more important to know what types of activities, programs, projects, or results the potential sponsor has funded in the past and plans to fund in the future that may match up nicely with the librarian's project idea. Many sponsors fund libraries within their complement of awarded nonprofit organizations.[1] A library's sponsorship team can begin searching for funding or in-kind contribution support by creating an Excel spreadsheet with columns for capturing information resulting from

FUNDING RESOURCES

Some examples of past CoLAB Planning Series Workshop sponsors include the following contributors of funding, food, space, or promotional activities.

Nonprofit and Private Philanthropic Support

ArtsServe (Broward County)
Community Foundation of Broward
Community Foundation for Palm Beach and Martin Counties
Glades Health Initiatives (Belle Glade, FL)
Junior League of Palm Beach County
Nonprofit Resource Center (Broward County)
Nonprofit Resource Institute (Palm Beach County)
Toward a New Perfect Union (Palm Beach County)
United Way of Martin County
United Way of Palm Beach County

Higher Education Support

Florida Atlantic University School of the Arts
Florida State University Libraries
University of Arizona BIO5
University of Arizona Libraries
University of Arizona McGuire Center for Entrepreneurship
University of Florida Center for the Humanities and the Public Sphere
University of Florida College of Arts
University of Florida College of Journalism and Communications
University of Florida Creative Campus Committee
University of Florida Department of Entomology
University of Florida Gallery

A QUICK TIP

When searching for corporate support guidelines or forms online, use key words like "community giving," "community service," "community grant program," or "sponsorship request." Often, a corporation will have various giving streams. For instance, when searching for the Chipotle application for a meal donation, use the search term "philanthropy," which leads to guidelines and an application for either a donation or a fundraiser using the link "Let's get in touch." Here is the website with the application: http://chipotle.com/email-us#philanthropy.

---

online searches, including the deadline, name of the sponsor, minimum and maximum amount of funding previously awarded, sponsor interests, and a link to the sponsor guidelines. Start by searching for sponsors within your local geographic area and then branch out to regional and national sponsors. Over time, the team will be able to accumulate a sufficient number of appropriate sponsors from which to solicit funding. Don't forget to include corporate sponsors that may provide workshop refreshments and meals, including Starbucks and Chipotle. Searching for funding opportunities can take time, but with a diligent weekly investment of one to two hours per week, the team will be surprised at the number of opportunities that may be a perfect fit.

Step 3: Prepare a Grant or Sponsorship Proposal

Preparing and submitting a proposal for funding or in-kind support can seem daunting, but seeking funding to present CoLAB Workshops has certain advantages. First, the team likely needs a small amount of funding (less than $15,000) to support four to

FUNDING RESOURCES (continued)

Higher Education Support (continued)

University of Florida Graduate School
University of Florida Health Science Center
University of Florida Libraries
University of North Texas Libraries
University of Washington Farm
University of Washington Dining
University of Washington Graduate School
University of Washington Information Technology
University of Washington Libraries
University of Washington Simpson Center for the Humanities
Women in Science and Engineering (University of Florida)

Government and Corporate Support

Children's Services Council (Broward County)
Children's Services Council (Palm Beach County)
City of Boynton Beach, Parks and Recreation Department
National Library of Medicine/National Institutes of Health
Procter & Gamble

Conferences

Association of Research Libraries Conference (Baltimore, MD)
College Book Arts Association 2017 Conference—Conspire: Collaboration, Cooperation, Collection (Tallahassee, FL)
Florida Library Association Conference (Orlando, FL)
Living the Future 7: Transforming Libraries through Collaboration (Tucson, AZ)

six workshops during a given year. Second, very few proposals can claim that the result of the proposed project will be at least ten to twenty partnerships that leverage extant community resources to extend outreach services, serve more clients, increase volunteerism, reduce redundancy of effort, or produce any number of possible cooperative, coordinative, collaborative, or mentorship benefits.

For instance, consider the following excerpt from a proposal submitted by the Smathers Libraries at the University of Florida to Procter & Gamble titled Collaborating with Strangers In and Outside Mass Communications:

> The George A. Smathers Libraries at the University of Florida (UF) respectfully request $4,292 to promote and facilitate the Collaborating with Strangers (CoLAB) networking workshops to connect 250 College of Journalism and Communications students, staff and faculty with others from business, engineering and health science colleges. Based on successful pilot workshops using the CoLAB Planning Series facilitation methods, participants will engage in 3-minute conversations with "strangers" on topics related to research, passions, skills and other "hidden" assets. An average of

50 participants per session will meet 12 to 20 strangers resulting in 5,000 possible total connections. The project goal is to use proven facilitation processes and online follow-up to eliminate networking barriers, while creating the fertile ground for creative, entrepreneurial ideas that arise from focused conversations between those in and outside the field of mass communications.[2]

Most funding guidelines will require the description of the project goals. The following excerpt provides more context for how to describe goals related to presenting a series of CoLAB Workshops:

1. Present five topic-based "Collaborating with Strangers" workshops . . . that connect students, staff and faculty in the UF College of Journalism and Communications with other disciplines such as business, engineering and the health sciences.
2. Improve interdisciplinary networking skills while participants increase their knowledge of available resources/assets using the CoLAB Planning Series speed-meeting process during each two-hour session.
3. Augment online community of participant profiles to encourage ongoing discovery and sharing of resources.
4. Promote process and results for future replications at other academic institutions through two conference presentations, publications and online research guide dedicated to collaboration and creativity.
5. Evaluate sessions through external evaluation services provided by David Miller, Ph.D., director of the College of Education's Collaborative Assessment and Program Evaluation Services, to determine effectiveness, improvements and components for replication.[3]

For workshops without a theme, consider the following text in a proposal that was submitted to the UF Creative Campus Committee for funding from the Catalyst Fund:

Collaborating with Strangers is a team effort by the UF Libraries (three librarians, PR officer, and grants manager/project facilitator) and partner representatives from arts, science, engineering, and various undergraduate programs to promote facilitate and evaluate 6 "speed meeting" sessions (2 hours each from 4 to 6 p.m.) based on a facilitative process known as CoLAB Planning. An average of 30 participants for each session will include faculty, graduate and undergraduate students; pre-registration is not required. External evaluation will determine effectiveness for future replication and expansion. The project goal is to use successful facilitation processes and online follow-up for eliminating barriers to networking and learning about extant campus resources. By doing so, the team and its partners will create the fertile ground necessary to generate creative ideas for sharing resources/ information while combining forces across disciplines.[4]

The project goals for this proposal included the following:

1. Utilize comfortable spaces in Marston Science Library, Library West, and University Gallery to create a safe and engaging environment for convening and connecting multiple disconnected campus audiences: undergrad/grad students and faculty from STEM and Arts disciplines, and undergraduate programs
2. Improve networking skills while revealing participants' hidden assets (passions, skills, resources, networks) using the CoLAB Planning speed-meeting process with a goal of recruiting 40 participants for each 2-hour session
3. Create an online community for further discovery and sharing of information
4. Evaluate sessions' effectiveness for improvements and replication[5]

Including statements that articulate the anticipated benefits of CoLAB Workshops within grant proposals will be an important component of any proposal. Sponsors often look for "broader impacts" that can be achieved beyond the direct benefits received during the CoLAB, for example:

> All participants will walk away with a renewed sense of community and access to this community. Sessions will create an energy of enthusiasm for learning from and about strangers, and will feel confident inquiring about access to new resources with any of the expected 240 participants. Simply identifying oneself as a "CoLABer" will grant permission to go beyond typical daily conversation, to a new level of confidence and inquiry required to seek resources and information.[6]

Step 4: Add CoLAB Workshops to Enhance Other Proposed Grant Projects

Project teams, in general, are often challenged by sponsoring agencies to include a partnership component within their proposals. Adding a presentation of a CoLAB Workshop or series of workshops to the list of proposed activities within a grant proposal on virtually any topic can improve the proposal's competitiveness. For instance, CoLAB Workshops have been included in several awarded grant proposals submitted by librarians at the UF Health Science Center Library and funded by the National Library of Medicine/National Institutes of Health.

One of the primary objectives of the Sex and Gender Differences/Women's Health Outreach Project, funded by the National Library of Medicine, was to facilitate collaboration development:

> Smathers Libraries personnel will lead two "Collaborating with Strangers" workshops using CoLAB Planning Series (CoLAB) facilitative processes for women's health and sex and gender differences researchers on UF's campus. These events are designed to introduce researchers to others in related fields

with whom they may be able to develop meaningful connections and to encourage interdisciplinary collaboration. Given the positive response from attendees at the two CoLAB sessions during the 2013 project, it is expected that these workshops will lead to new and innovative research projects in women's health and sex and gender differences.[7]

Once the CoLAB team members have sufficient experience promoting and facilitating workshops, they will be prepared to offer these services to others in their communities. Using a CoLAB Workshop as an option for meeting requirements of community engagement or collaboration activities within a grant proposal can be the key to ensuring the proposal is considered innovative and collaborative. Making your library colleagues, academic faculty, and nonprofit organization administrators aware of this possibility can lead to many more grant awards for your community.

NOTES

1. Bess G. de Farber, *Collaborative Grant-Seeking: A Practical Guide for Librarians* (Lanham, MD: Rowman & Littlefield, 2016), 67.
2. April Hines and Bess de Farber, "Collaborating with Strangers In and Outside Mass Communications: Procter & Gamble" (PDF document, 2013), http://ufdc.ufl.edu/AA00019151/00001, 2.
3. April Hines, "Mini Grant: 'Collaborating with Strangers In and Outside Mass Communications': Mini Grant Application Packet" (PDF document, October 2013), http://ufdc.ufl.edu/IR00003574/00001, 2.
4. Missy Clapp, Bess de Farber, Barbara Hood et al., "Collaborating with Strangers (CoLAB) Grant Proposal" (PDF document, 2011), http://ufdc.ufl.edu/AA00013651/00002, 1.
5. Ibid.
6. Ibid., 1, 3.
7. Michele Tennant, Mary Edwards, Hannah Norton et al., "Sex and Gender Differences/Women's Health Outreach Project" (PDF document, 2014), http://ufdc.ufl.edu/AA00019464/00001, 1

Promotional Strategies for CoLAB Workshops

Other than in classroom or conference settings that don't require recruitment efforts, CoLAB Workshops must be promoted to attract attendees. This chapter presents detailed descriptions of the four major strategies involved in promoting a workshop or a series of workshops.

Designing Promotional Materials

Promotional materials are an indispensable component of creating successful CoLAB Workshop experiences. The unusual challenges presented by these workshops dictate that sufficient time be set aside to produce these materials. The length of time of a typical CoLAB Workshop, the sharing of personal information, and the activity of wearing a profile-sign during the speed-meeting process may present issues that can inhibit or discourage some from participating. The suggestions that follow for designing promotional materials will help to mitigate these concerns.

An attractive, easy-to-read postcard or flyer, in print and electronic formats, that can be widely distributed is key to attracting workshop participants. Here are the steps for planning and executing these formats.

Step 1: Choose an image to represent the workshop.

After determining the workshop title, date, time, and location, as described in chapter 4, the first step is to choose an image that represents the title to use on printed pieces, in electronic announcements, and on social media.

The purpose of the image is to brand the workshop at first glance. The image must relate to the subject of the workshop. For a workshop focused on a theme such as grant seeking, the team should brainstorm the types of images that convey the topic. These might include a lightbulb that represents new ideas or dollar signs and the color green to represent money. (See figure 7.1.)

FIGURE 7.1

PROMOTIONAL IMAGE FOR GRANTS SEEKERS CoLAB

Design by
Barbara Hood

Another example might be a workshop intended to attract students who are interested in mass communications. The team could identify the disciplines within mass communications that they want to attract to the workshop and find an image that represents those areas. In this case, the disciplines could include advertising, journalism, public relations, telecommunications, science/health communication, social media, and web design. In figure 7.2, you will notice these areas are represented by a variety of appropriate icons.

FIGURE 7.2

PROMOTIONAL IMAGE FOR MASS COMMUNICATIONS CoLAB

Design by
Barbara Hood

Experiment to determine which image will best grab attention. Look for copyright-free images. Examples of websites that the team might find helpful in looking for suitable images include the following:

- All-Free-Download.com, "Free Vectors" (http://all-free-download.com/free-vector): These vector images can be enlarged without losing resolution.
- Google Images (https://images.google.com): For images that can be used anywhere, click on search tools and then click "usage rights" and select an option, such as "Labeled for reuse with modification."
- Image Chef (www.imagechef.com): The team can use this site to modify and create low-resolution free images that can be used for electronic announcements. However, the images may not be suitable for printing.

If an image is not available to represent the CoLAB Workshop topic, or if there is no featured topic, another option is to create a word cloud using a program like Wordle (www.wordle.net). Simply brainstorm all of the keywords that would describe the types of organizations or students the team intends to attract. Terms could include arts, culture, science, museum, ballet, sculpture, theatre, concerts, music, performances, education, and so forth. For those workshops intended to attract participants who work or study in close proximity to one another, select words like innovate, collaborate, coordinate, cooperate, merge, invent, create, connect, and other terms that describe the workshop's intended results. These Wordle images provide a good substitute for that illusive "pre-packaged" image that doesn't quite communicate the workshop's intent.

Step 2: Select the software to use and determine the format for promotional materials.

If the team doesn't have access to professional graphics software such as Adobe InDesign, alternative options include Microsoft PowerPoint or Publisher to design the materials. Microsoft Word will suffice if that is the CoLAB team's only option. In that case, make the design as simple as possible.

At this point, the team is prepared to determine the type of promotional materials and the respective sizes for the print versions. If the promotional materials will be electronic, then the team should determine an appropriate file size for reliable e-mail distribution.

Step 3: Design and create the promotional materials.

Promotional materials should use no more than two fonts. For the workshop title, choose a large, casual, fun, bold font and a secondary smaller, easy-to-read font for the remainder of the text, including date, time, location, and other workshop descriptive details.

If the team plans to present a series of workshops, then use the same fonts and font sizes each time workshops are promoted to build identity and recognition. Many free font websites are available for downloading fonts, such as DaFont.com (www.dafont.com) or 100FreeFonts.com (www.100freefonts.com).

In the body of promotional materials, be sure to include who, what, when, where, why, and how to register within the text. If refreshments or a meal will be served, include this information also, along with all appropriate logos and sponsor names. The team should consider the type of participants they want to attract. When presenting a CoLAB Workshop on a college campus for students, faculty, and staff, it is important to communicate the "fun" and innovative nature of this real-time collaboration workshop experience. For instance, using the style of text shown in figure 7.3 may yield the most participation.

Finally, choose colors that best represent the topic of the workshop. The color red can represent HIV/AIDS prevention and services, as symbolized by the iconic red ribbon. For a grant-seeking theme, the postcard could use green as its main color, and green also can be used to promote grant-seeking and sustainability-themed workshop materials.

Combining all of the elements into a single graphic image provides the team with the ability to repurpose the content to create three distinct products: a printed postcard, a printed poster, and an e-postcard. Figure 7.4 presents an annotated postcard that explains the individual design elements the team should consider. For more examples of promotional materials, see the document "CoLAB Workshops Promotional Materials" (http://ufdc.ufl.edu//IR00008407/00001).

FIGURE 7.3

PROMOTIONAL TEXT FOR POSTCARD AND POSTER

orator. You are more creative than you think. The inspiration you've been looking for is right around the corner.

You will soon meet a future collaborator.

Potential, you must first meet each other.

Hey stranger.

...looking for a way to turn small talk into big ideas?
Collaborating with Strangers Workshops are designed to connect students, faculty and researchers on campus during 3-minute speed-meetings. You'll walk away with more resources, solutions and creative ideas than you could have ever imagined.

When: Wednesday, April 4, 2012 – 4:00-5:30 p.m.
Where: Marston Science Library, main floor
Who: All University of Florida students and faculty

Visit **www.uflib.ufl.edu/pio/colab/home.html** for information and registration.

Cookies and beverages will be served.

UF | George A. Smathers Libraries | UNIVERSITY *of* FLORIDA

If you want to go fast go alone.
If you want to go far go together.

Co-sponsored by I-Cubed, College of Engineering, College of Fine Arts, Honors Program, the UF Graduate School, Florida Opportunities Scholars Program and Women in Science and Engineering. **Funded by the Creative Campus Committee Catalyst Fund.**

one person. Bigger ideas come from two. An unexpected stranger will become your teammate. To reach your

Someone will soon help you solve an old problem. Big ideas come from

Text by Bess de Farber and Logan Jaffe

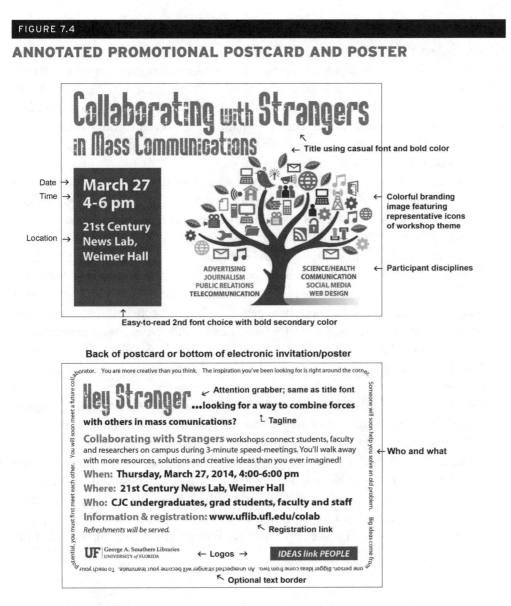

FIGURE 7.4

ANNOTATED PROMOTIONAL POSTCARD AND POSTER

Design by Barbara Hood

Pushing Out the Promotional Materials

If using printed postcards or flyers, make color copies on your printer or take the file to a copy center. Then distribute to all appropriate locations. The design for the electronic announcements can be exported as a JPEG and embedded into an e-mail message that team members can send to all potential workshop participants. Directly ask the recipients to share the message with others whom they think would be interested. Always be sure to include a link for registration.

The team also should consider crafting an e-mail message for distribution by the workshop's sponsors and other interested constituent groups. Identify organizations, associations, and groups that maintain ongoing lists of members or affiliated individuals. For example, in a campus environment, to reach faculty and students, e-mail discussion lists managed by the graduate school or a specific campus unit can serve as vehicles to help widely distribute the message. To broaden the reach of promotion in a nonprofit sector, contact the local Community Foundation, United Way, homeless coalition, Children's Services Council, or arts agency, all of which are engaged in strengthening collaborative ties among their local grantees and other organizations. With the distribution of promotional materials through these agencies, the workshops themselves will receive credibility and endorsement. Expanding the reach through other e-mail discussion lists and organizations ensures the possibility of a wider and more diverse group of potential workshop participants.

Social media outlets can greatly broaden the reach of the workshop promotional message. Posting multiple times to the host organization's and the team's individual social media accounts, using the color art image or the entire electronic announcement, is a casual method for disseminating an upcoming workshop message. If the host organization is on Facebook, an event page can be created specifically for every workshop.

Creating and distributing a traditional news release should be considered if the workshop is open to the public or to nonprofit organization representatives. On campus, a news article published in the campus newspaper can be an effective means of attracting participants from specific disciplines, for workshops with a theme, or for general audience participation. Include a link to the electronic postcard in case the editor wants to publish the workshop icon image. Figure 7.5 is an example of a news release sent to a campus newspaper.

The article shown in figure 7.6 was published by *The Independent Florida Alligator* for promoting an upcoming workshop to the University of Florida community.

Additional tools for building credibility and awareness of the CoLAB Workshop processes include producing conference posters, for example, at state or national library or education conferences, publishing academic papers (e.g., see "Results from the ACRL Scholarly Communication 101 Road Show, and CoLAB Planning Session," http://ufdc .ufl.edu/IR00009132/00001), and publishing articles in community newsletters (e.g., see "Making an Impact—Our Future's Promise," www.jlbr.org/wp-content/uploads/2005 -January.pdf, p. 22).

Designing a Dedicated CoLAB Workshop Website

If the host organization plans to present multiple CoLAB Workshops, then it is advantageous to consider setting up a dedicated website. The website will communicate the host organization's long-term commitment to presenting CoLAB Workshops on a regular basis, thus building a brand and recognizable program for facilitating collaboration development. A website also will provide a vehicle for attracting potential workshop participants and for sharing examples of past workshops.

The home page can display the workshop icon image or images for upcoming workshops with an embedded registration link. It also can include icons or links to secondary pages, such as "Meet the Participants," "Idea Boards," "Evaluation Reports," "Testimonials," "Sponsors," "Resources," "Process," "Workshop Photos," "Registration," and "Contact Information." Many of the secondary pages should link to each individual workshop image. Here are examples of the kinds of content that can be found on each webpage:

FIGURE 7.5

NEWS RELEASE PROMOTING SUSTAINABILITY CoLAB AT UF

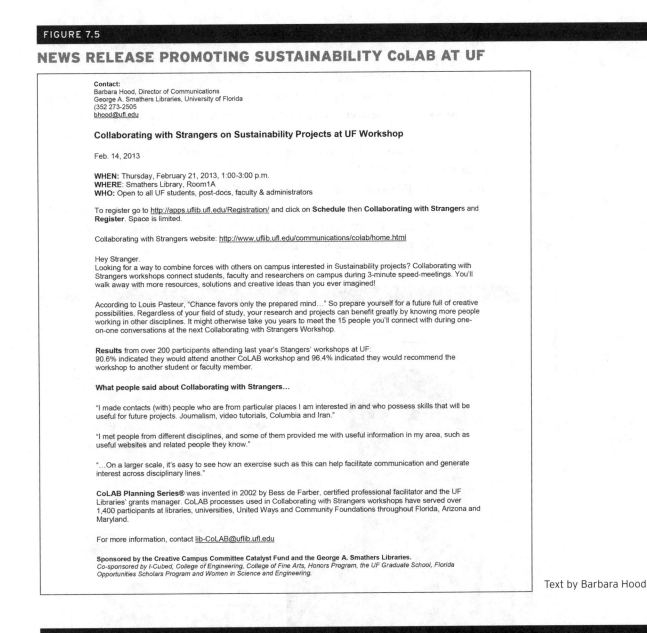

Contact:
Barbara Hood, Director of Communications
George A. Smathers Libraries, University of Florida
(352 273-2505
bhood@ufl.edu

Collaborating with Strangers on Sustainability Projects at UF Workshop

Feb. 14, 2013

WHEN: Thursday, February 21, 2013, 1:00-3:00 p.m.
WHERE: Smathers Library, Room1A
WHO: Open to all UF students, post-docs, faculty & administrators

To register go to http://apps.uflib.ufl.edu/Registration/ and click on **Schedule** then **Collaborating with Strangers** and **Register**. Space is limited.

Collaborating with Strangers website: http://www.uflib.ufl.edu/communications/colab/home.html

Hey Stranger.
Looking for a way to combine forces with others on campus interested in Sustainability projects? Collaborating with Strangers workshops connect students, faculty and researchers on campus during 3-minute speed-meetings. You'll walk away with more resources, solutions and creative ideas than you ever imagined!

According to Louis Pasteur, "Chance favors only the prepared mind…" So prepare yourself for a future full of creative possibilities. Regardless of your field of study, your research and projects can benefit greatly by knowing more people working in other disciplines. It might otherwise take you years to meet the 15 people you'll connect with during one-on-one conversations at the next Collaborating with Strangers Workshop.

Results from over 200 participants attending last year's Stangers' workshops at UF:
90.6% indicated they would attend another CoLAB workshop and 96.4% indicated they would recommend the workshop to another student or faculty member.

What people said about Collaborating with Strangers…

"I made contacts (with) people who are from particular places I am interested in and who possess skills that will be useful for future projects. Journalism, video tutorials, Columbia and Iran."

"I met people from different disciplines, and some of them provided me with useful information in my area, such as useful websites and related people they know."

"…On a larger scale, it's easy to see how an exercise such as this can help facilitate communication and generate interest across disciplinary lines."

CoLAB Planning Series® was invented in 2002 by Bess de Farber, certified professional facilitator and the UF Libraries' grants manager. CoLAB processes used in Collaborating with Strangers workshops have served over 1,400 participants at libraries, universities, United Ways and Community Foundations throughout Florida, Arizona and Maryland.

For more information, contact lib-CoLAB@uflib.ufl.edu

Sponsored by the Creative Campus Committee Catalyst Fund and the George A. Smathers Libraries.
Co-sponsored by I-Cubed, College of Engineering, College of Fine Arts, Honors Program, the UF Graduate School, Florida Opportunities Scholars Program and Women in Science and Engineering.

Text by Barbara Hood

FIGURE 7.6

NEWSPAPER ARTICLE ABOUT SEX AND GENDER DIFFERENCES IN HEALTH CoLAB

Event hopes to spark sex conversation

❭ **IT'S TUESDAY IN THE MCKNIGHT BRAIN INSTITUTE.**

MELISSA FIGUEROA
Alligator Contributing Writer

On Tuesday from 2:30 until 4:30 p.m., the Health Science Center Libraries will be hosting Collaborating with Strangers on Sex and Gender Differences in Health, a CoLAB geared toward developing cross-disciplinary conversations and solutions for health sciences.

"In a year, you may have 12 con-versations with someone you don't know. With a coLAB, you can have 12 to 17 conversations in a matter of two hours," said Bess de Farber, grants manager for the Smathers Libraries.

Participants fill out a profile board with personal information that they wear throughout the night. Having the boards facilitates better discussion, she said.

In three-minute increments, participants go around and meet different people and talk about sex and gender differences, de Farber said.

"I call it speed-meeting," she said.

Participants are UF faculty, staff and students from all colleges and departments on campus.

"Many students came away with potential mentors or internships, and faculty left with new collaborators on their research, regardless of discipline," said Hannah Norton, reference and liaison librarian for the Health Science Center Libraries.

Collaborating with Strangers on Sex and Gender Differences in Health will be in the McKnight Brain Institute, Room L6-110 A/B.

Text by Melissa Figueroa, http://ufdc.ufl.edu/ UF00028290/01743

123

- "Meet the Participants": Participant headshots and accompanying profile-signs should be posted to this page (e.g., see figure 7.7). Each workshop participant's headshot and scanned profile-sign will serve to remind attendees of whom they spoke to and those they might want to contact for an initial conversation. Headshots and profile-signs from previous workshops also are displayed for browsing and potential partnerships. Each of the workshops can be linked to and from the workshop icon image as a means for distinguishing each workshop (see figure 7.8.)
- "Idea Boards": Responses gathered from the three Idea Boards can be transcribed for use as content on this webpage, featuring participant feedback and ideas. The Idea Board responses can be linked to the workshop icon image as a means for workshop identification. (See figure 7.9.)

FIGURE 7.7

PARTICIPANT AND PROFILE-SIGN ON WEBSITE

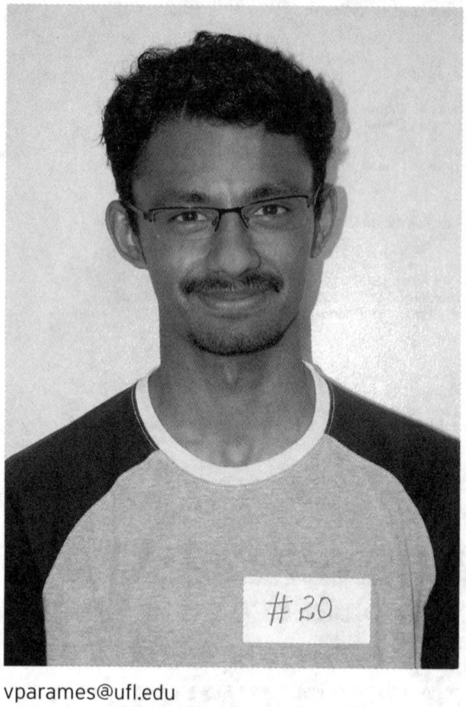

First Name: VENKITACHALAM
Hometown/state/country: TAMIL NADU, INDIA
Department or research area: MECHANICAL ENGINEERING
#20

☐ Faculty ☑ Graduate Student ☐ Undergraduate Student ☐ Other

What is your area of study or research interest and why are you passionate about this work?
PARALLEL MANIPULATORS, AUTOMATION CREATING AUTOMATED TECHNOLOGY MAKING HUMAN LIFE EASIER HAS ALWAYS FASCINATED ME.

What are your strongest skills? (narrative or list)
LEADERSHIP
CREATIVITY
ORGANIZING TECHNICAL & CULTURAL EVENTS
(PRAAARSHA - 2012)

What grants have you applied for or plan to apply for?
NONE SO FAR.

What groups or networks are you involved in or support? (narrative or list)
ASHA UFLORIDA - WEBMASTER
FUNDRAISER
IGSA
GRADUATE STUDENT COUNCIL

What's one thing that most people don't know about you?
I CREATE DIGITAL ART
WEB DESIGNER
SOFTWARE DEVELOPER

vparames@ufl.edu

Document by Venkitachalam Parameswaran

FIGURE 7.8

SCREENSHOT OF WORKSHOP MENU ON WEBSITE

FIGURE 7.9

SCREENSHOT OF "IDEA BOARDS" PAGE ON WEBSITE

- "Evaluation Reports": To display the results from past workshops, consider linking the actual evaluation reports on the evaluation page of the website, arranged by workshop date and title. The team can select samples of interesting facts from reports to share snapshots of the key "takeaways" experienced by participants. Exposing these reports also gives workshops an added layer of credibility. (See figure 7.10.)
- "Testimonials": For this content, the team can mine statements made by participants through the Idea Boards and postworkshop surveys. Inevitably, every CoLAB Workshop will produce a variety of comments that highlight its value from several different perspectives. Having these thoughts and comments in writing can help future workshop participants answer the universal question, "What's in it for me?" (See figure 7.11.)
- "Sponsors": This webpage can highlight logos representing those that provided in-kind contributions like refreshments, space, or promotional assistance, as well as funding for necessary workshop components. Posting sponsorship logos on the CoLAB website also can serve as a vehicle for advertising those businesses or community groups that support these workshops, thus bolstering the credibility of the workshops.
- "Resources": Especially for topic-based CoLAB Workshops, there often will be additional resources that participants might want to access for follow-up. This can be in the form of a bibliography; links to online articles, videos, or books; or other community resources.
- "Process": Sharing information about the history of facilitated activities presented during CoLAB Workshops (see chapter 2) can provide context for those who may want to request a workshop. This history also can serve as a recruitment tool. Understanding how these workshops came to be developed, the number of people and organizations that have benefited, and the kinds of connections that have resulted will help to paint the picture for future participants and sponsors.
- "Workshop Photos": During the workshop, especially the speed-meetings, make sure one of the team members is assigned to take photographs. Speed-meeting conversations may present several challenges for the photographer because people are matched in pairs and their backs will create barriers to viewing the activity in the image. Try standing on a chair to get full overview shots of the process. Or you can limit the number of pairs within an image to just one or a few. Make sure you move around the room while activities are happening to try to capture as many participants in action as possible. Try to avoid creating a distraction. This can be a particularly salient consideration if media representatives are covering the event.
- "Registration": Visitors to the website should be able to easily locate the registration link. It can have its own tab as well as a hyperlink to the workshop promotional image.
- "Contact Information": The team should consider creating a dedicated e-mail address for ongoing CoLAB Workshop correspondence. This is another way to brand these collaboration workshops as an ongoing program.

After the completion of each workshop, headshot photos with accompanying scanned profile-signs along with photographs taken during the workshop process and a

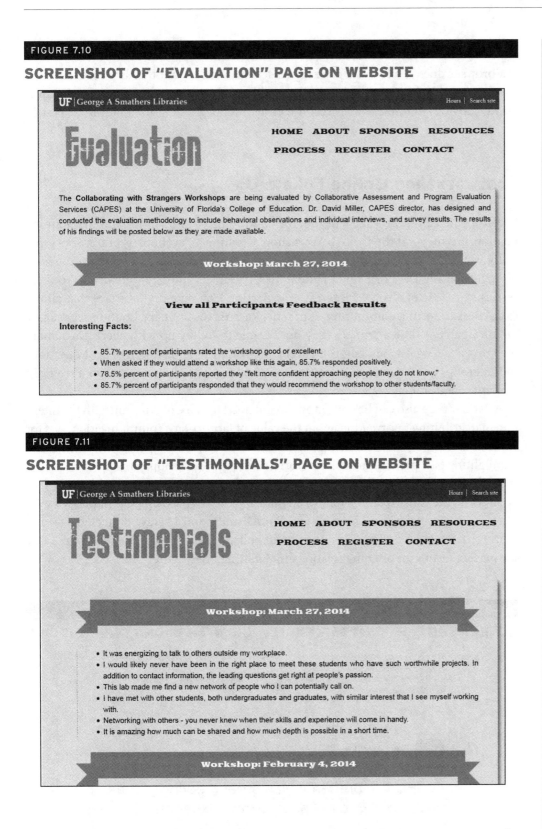

FIGURE 7.10

SCREENSHOT OF "EVALUATION" PAGE ON WEBSITE

FIGURE 7.11

SCREENSHOT OF "TESTIMONIALS" PAGE ON WEBSITE

transcription of the Idea Board responses can be loaded to the appropriate pages on the website. Once completed, send the link(s) to the workshop photos and other workshop results to the participants as described in chapter 4. If the team does not plan to use a website to capture this content, the scanned images can be combined into a document, saved to PDF format, and then sent to the participants.

An alternative is to convert the PDF document into a flipbook at https://issuu.com. If a browser doesn't allow the page turner to function, try another browser. The Collaborating with Strangers website (www.uflib.ufl.edu/communications/colab/home .html) provides examples of the recommended webpages described in this chapter.

Postworkshop Online Follow-Up

Social media can be an excellent tool for continuing conversations and maintaining relationships beyond the CoLAB Workshop. Creating a Facebook group works especially well for those who attended a topic-based session, such as Collaborating with Strangers on Big Data or Digital Humanities. Attendees initially were drawn to these sessions because of a shared interest or expertise. Having a digital space that allows CoLABers to form a community of practice (across disciplinary boundaries) can be quite valuable. While attendees may not be able to follow up with every participant they met at a CoLAB Workshop, a Facebook group will allow them to post questions to the group, link to articles or new resources, and upload documents in a friendly, informal environment.

A Twitter page also can be created and maintained by the CoLAB team with the intention of distributing information about the value of face-to-face communication, tips for enhancing creativity and innovation, upcoming CoLAB Workshop announcements, and highlighting past participant success stories. During a workshop, participants also can share their own social media handles directly on their profile-signs, and these can then be added to the CoLAB online follow-up information. If a participant is impressed with a certain individual whom they met at a CoLAB and wants to stay connected—even if they don't see an immediate opportunity for collaboration—social media can provide the perfect forum for ongoing relationship building. (See figure 7.12.)

FIGURE 7.12

SCREENSHOT OF TWITTER EXCHANGE WITH CoLAB PARTICIPANT

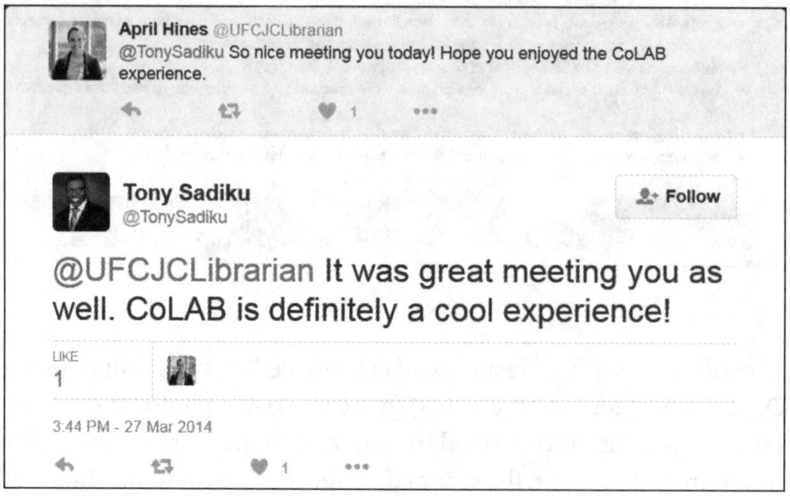

April Hines @UFCJCLibrarian
@TonySadiku So nice meeting you today! Hope you enjoyed the CoLAB experience.

Tony Sadiku
@TonySadiku

&+ Follow

@UFCJCLibrarian It was great meeting you as well. CoLAB is definitely a cool experience!

LIKE
1

3:44 PM - 27 Mar 2014

Tips and Lessons Learned for Presenting Successful CoLAB Workshops

IN THIS CHAPTER
✓ Recommendations and Best Practices
✓ Envisioning the Future

The activities related to presenting CoLAB Workshops—planning agendas, preparing supplies, facilitating participants, and following up after the workshop—can make it appear that there are lots of moving parts. Regardless, the one thing to keep in mind is that you want the experiences associated with these workshops to be consistently positive for all participants, requesters, and sponsors.

This chapter highlights recommendations and best practices that support the CoLAB team's intention to make each participant and stakeholder feel valued throughout his or her engagement in a CoLAB Workshop or process. It is equally important to ensure that the team members themselves enjoy the experience of managing and facilitating workshops. The chapter also offers solutions to some common situations that can occur during the planning or conducting of CoLAB Workshops, for example:

- Unwillingness to participate or share personal information
- The need to alter the format of the CoLAB Workshop
- Food and drink considerations
- Accommodating persons with disabilities
- More or fewer participants than are registered
- Late arrivals and early departures
- Participants' predetermined expectations
- Participant confusion about the purpose of the workshop
- Participants not following speed-meeting instructions
- Odd number of participants during speed-meetings
- Incomplete evaluation surveys or permission forms
- Difficulties engaging participants postworkshop

Based on past workshop experiences, the recommendations that follow will help in preparing team members to address these typical circumstances with calmness and grace.

Recommendations and Best Practices

Emphasize that participation is voluntary and allow participants to choose how much and what they want to share.

CoLAB Workshop participation, except as part of a required class activity, should not be compulsory. As mentioned previously, CoLAB Workshops are based on the principle that participants must self-select to participate. This means that, in general, they should have a genuine interest or curiosity in engaging with other potential partners and in learning from the overall workshop experience. The presence of a single participant who has registered because his or her attendance has been made a requirement in an employment situation can introduce a counterproductive sense of negativity. Most of the time, such participants can see the benefits in a CoLAB Workshop and become swept up by the rapid conversations and the quick selection of new partners. But those few who truly do not want to engage in conversations or don't see the point will be partnering with at least eleven others in one-to-one conversations, and thereby spreading a sense of dissatisfaction with the facilitated process.

The way to eliminate the very few disgruntled participants is to be consistent in the messaging related to the workshop with everyone involved, including the requester and, of course, all those who inquire about the workshop itself. The message should be that every aspect of the workshop is voluntary. If for any reason there is some discomfort when it comes to sponsorship, hosting, or participation, then it is best to reconsider the commitment or to make adjustments for individual needs to be met, whatever they may be.

For example, let's say that a participant doesn't want to share a lot of information on his or her profile-sign. A facilitator's response should be to encourage the participant to share only that information which he or she is willing to share. Providing an example of a fully completed profile-sign can help to inspire the sharing of more information. Some participants may simply be very cautious about sharing personal information. Others may have difficulty when it comes to acknowledging and/or sharing their assets. They may be modest, or they may not have an inherent understanding of their own self-worth.

You may wonder whether the speed-meetings will be successful if a few people barely share any information at all. In the case of participants who are not representing an organization, this can work just fine. They may have shared enough information to support three- to four-minute speed-meeting conversations. Simply including the name of one's hometown on a profile-sign can be sufficient.

Another possible challenge for participants who are not representing organizations is the reluctance to allow their headshots to be taken. This might be overcome by helping them to understand the purpose of the headshots, which is solely to allow for postworkshop online access via a secure webpage or PDF to view the headshots. Participants will be more easily able to recall whether they conversed with individuals if headshots are available. Those who want to protect their identities or who don't want their individual photos taken should be encouraged to participate regardless. They can be instructed to write "NP" (no photo) on their profile-signs to let the workshop team know that headshots were not taken. Facilitators should communicate that it is fine to skip the headshot, to minimize any discomfort a participant may have about declining. A headshot can be taken even after the speed-meeting process if the participant changes his or her mind and wants a headshot to be shared. Demonstrating to participants that the facilitators are flexible and consistently positive in their enthusiasm for the workshop and its processes can contribute greatly to creating an environment that is comfortable and supportive, regardless of the situation.

Stay true to the format of the CoLAB Workshop.

Any major alteration to the agenda that might divert, dilute, or delay the focus of the workshop activities should be minimized. For instance, a requester's insistence that the workshop include guest speakers related to the topic has the potential to change the inherent nature of the workshop itself. Beyond the introductory PowerPoint presentation about partnership strategies, asset-based community development, and ways to enhance creativity, CoLAB Workshops are intended to avoid the traditional lecture or presentation style of delivering content to a quiet audience. Generally, participants' primary reason for attending a CoLAB Workshop is to participate in speed-meetings. The facilitators should expect some frustration if this process is delayed to allow one or two "experts" to impart their knowledge, experiences, or beliefs about the topic of the workshop.

Be flexible with regard to time constraints.

Let's say that a requester can accommodate only a forty-five-minute session. Rather than declining the request, revise a workshop agenda to include a shorter presentation and use the icebreaker version of the workshop described in chapter 4.

Provide refreshments that suit the type and length of the workshop.

The purpose of a CoLAB is to connect with others. Unlike some meetings, food is not the motivation to attend. Not only is there very little time for eating, but experience has shown that participants are not interested in eating during CoLAB activities. If you put out a big spread as the main attraction, you likely will have most of it left over. Bottled water is a must, however, and participants may be grateful to have some cookies close by. But unless a meal is scheduled during the workshop or there is a long break to share ideas at tables, having food in the room is at best a distraction.

Plan to accommodate persons with varying disabilities.

The team should be prepared to accommodate persons with varying disabilities during a workshop. Let's consider the needs of those who are visually or hearing impaired. If a registrant has a visual or hearing impairment, then the team should recommend that the registrant be accompanied by someone who will be available to attend the entire

LESSON LEARNED

Encouraging participation by library staff, who will provide on-the-fly resources and referrals, adds value to any CoLAB.

LESSON LEARNED

No two workshops will be the same. Allow for flexibility during the workshop.

LESSON LEARNED

Participants will invent their own methods for interacting with strangers during the speed-meetings. Some will sit in one place and partners will naturally come to them. Some may feel challenged to generate questions during speed-meetings and thus be more comfortable just responding to partners' questions. Others may want to find quiet spaces to meet with their partners.

131

workshop and provide ongoing interpretation. During speed-meetings, it should be easy for the participant to wear the profile-sign and, along with his or her assistant, move through the session to meet the other participants. The interpreter can "read" the sign to the participant as he or she moves from partner to partner or interpret the conversation as needed. If the registrant cannot provide an interpreter, it would be up to the team to provide one.

For those who are wheelchair bound or have other physical limitations, the speed-meetings are designed to accommodate this type of disability. The room should be arranged in such a way that allows someone in a wheelchair the ease of moving around the room without obstructions. In other cases where the participant has less mobility, during the speed-meeting process, partners will naturally move to those whom they have not met yet, whether they remain seated or stand in one location the entire time without moving. In fact, many times, participants have sat through the entire speed-meeting process, comfortably waiting for their next partner to locate them during each round. It happens without any additional effort.

Have contingency plans for accommodating more or fewer participants than expected.

Fewer than fourteen participants arrive.

You have some options: (1) Ask for a show of hands from those who want to hear the presentation and participate in a few rounds of speed-meetings as more of a workshop demonstration than a full CoLAB Workshop experience. You also can offer the speed-meetings to lengthen the workshop and form Idea Tables where participants can share what they discovered or why they registered for the workshop. If you have unanimous agreement, then proceed. (2) Ask for forgiveness, but cancel the workshop and reschedule it, maybe using a Doodle poll (www.doodle.com), based on attendees' schedules, granting them the security of a future date and time when they will be available. Ensure you have everyone's contact information before they leave.

More participants show up than the number who registered.

This is fine, as long as you have enough supplies to handle the overflow and enough seats and tables for participants to prepare their profile-signs. It's always a good idea to have more supplies than you think you will need.

Fewer participants show up than the number who registered.

At an academic institution, it is typical that out of those who have registered for the workshop, only one-half or one-third will actually show up. This should be the team's premise from the outset if the library is hosting the event. If another academic unit has requested a CoLAB Workshop and the team has agreed that the requester will guarantee at least fourteen participants, then this relieves the team of the marketing requirement.

Accommodate participants who arrive late.

Late arrivals are not a problem unless their tardiness prohibits them from partnering in the workshop speed-meetings. If it looks like there is insufficient time for late participants to prepare their profile-signs and jump into at least two rounds of meeting conversations, then it's best if they try to attend another workshop in the future.

Explain the ambiguous nature of the workshop.

Some participants will arrive with predetermined expectations. This may be challenging to mitigate unless the facilitator asks this leading question during the presentation: "Does anyone have a specific goal in mind that they hope to achieve during the session?" After hands are raised, the facilitator can reiterate that the team's goal is simply to provide a forum where connections can be made or resources can be discovered. Share that it is somewhat of an ambiguous process and that it is best to stay open to all the possibilities rather than to look for the "needle in a haystack." For example, a faculty member who is searching for a statistical analyst to help with a data-mining project may be disappointed after the workshop if his or her initial expectations are not met. Regardless, the faculty member may have been successful in acquiring knowledge of new campus resources or received feedback on ways to improve classroom engagement among his or her students. In situations like these, the CoLAB team can emphasize the importance of accepting the ambiguity created by the workshop, which can produce unexpected benefits.

Be clear about the purpose of the workshop.

Participants may be confused about the purpose of the workshop if the requester or promoter misunderstands the purpose of a CoLAB Workshop and passes on incorrect or inconsistent information to workshop registrants. For example, in a workshop for a public relations class tasked with creating a campus-wide campaign focused on internationalization, the CoLAB team was invited to present a session where they anticipated students would be sharing their own experiences with internationalization in an effort to inspire branding messages and other creative ideas from a student perspective. After a brief meeting with the instructor, the CoLAB team assumed that all parties had agreed on the same vision. However, students simply were told that they would be attending a session where they would receive assistance in developing their campaign projects. The students showed up expecting hands-on assistance in finding resources and crafting their campaign strategies. Upon realizing the actual intent of the session, students seemed confused about why they were there. Clear communication with the requester ahead of time and also with those registering for the workshop should prevent this kind of misunderstanding from happening.

LESSON LEARNED

The ambiguity of the CoLAB process can make some participants uncomfortable, initially, until they discover some connections and resources of value.

LESSON LEARNED

Watch participants and listen to the volume of speed-meetings. If it looks like participants are growing quieter or moving slower, it may mean that they need a break, water, or a cookie.

LESSON LEARNED

If the goal is that all participants will meet everyone in the CoLAB, expect that toward the end of the speed-meeting rounds, partnering with new strangers will become increasingly difficult as the pool of haven't-met-strangers decreases.

133

Be flexible about group composition.

Let's say that the workshop goal is to bring together two different groups, but the number of participants representing one group clearly exceeds the other. Before the speed-meeting process begins, have members of each group raise their hands to count the number of participants. Then share this finding with attendees. Indicate that because there are sufficient numbers of participants to run the workshop, the facilitators will proceed with the hope that those representing the larger group will have new things to learn and discover from those they may already "know."

Use gentle reminders and offer options to control particpants' behavior during speed-meetings.

During the speed-meetings, too many participants apparently are not reading their partners' signs.

You can tell when this is happening by the lack of a period of relative silence during which participants should be reading the new profile-signs after everyone has moved to a new partner. If you hear nonstop talking from the start of the speed-meeting round's stopwatch until the bell has been rung, then many participants probably are ignoring the signs. In this situation, a facilitator can make an emphatic announcement, between rounds, to remind participants to "read the profile-signs." Another option is to temporarily stop the workshop by speaking into the microphone or using a whistle to stop the process; then politely indicate the observation that profile-signs are not being read by many participants, quickly explain why this is an important step, and resume the process.

Some pairs don't decouple during speed-meetings when time is up.

Facilitators should expect that there will be a few participants who cannot end their speed-meeting conversations when the bell is rung. In these situations, facilitators should avoid creating any negativity around this occurrence. In fact, the team should plan strategies ahead of time for how they will deal with those who don't or can't move when they hear the bell. Here are some suggestions.

If, in the first few rounds of speed-meetings, a pair hasn't moved and everyone else already has paired up with a new partner, a facilitator can try to accommodate the pair who didn't move by finding another pair and interrupting the beginning of their conversation. Ask, "Would it be okay with both of you to split up and start again with new partners?" The answer has always been yes. Facilitators also can describe this scenario prior to sharing the facetious oath (see chapter 4) as a means for introducing the "problem" and describing the facilitated "solution" so participants can anticipate that this interruption might happen often throughout the session.

If a pair hasn't moved to new partners, but this occurs during the end of the speed-meeting process and there are very few strangers left in the room to choose from, the solution may be to (1) have the pair continue their conversation for another round, (2) have them pair up with workshop team members who have completed their profile-signs and are prepared to jump into the speed-meeting process, (3) split the pair and facilitate each one joining another pair to form two groups of three participants, with at least one person they have not yet met, or (4) allow the pair to sit out one round and enjoy a cookie.

The team should not be so concerned with pairs detaching and finding new partners that they make participants nervous about not finishing their conversations when the bells are rung. Sometimes just ringing the bell until everyone has changed partners is the best option. Or speaking into the microphone while the bell is ringing to say, "You must move, you must move, you must move . . ." will help them. A facilitator might even add a touch of levity in his or her tone of voice or commentary at this point. It may seem rude to cut off conversations, but there is no time for graciousness when everyone else in the workshop has found a new partner except a single pair of participants. Solutions like hovering over participants, getting in their space by nudging them physically or verbally to move, or deciding for participants whom they should partner with next can turn a perfectly relaxed and comfortable environment into a frenzied one.

Have team members who are ready to join speed-meeting conversations as needed.

Sometimes during the speed-meetings there will be an odd number of participants. The solution to this situation is to always have at least one CoLAB team member ready to grab his or her profile-sign and jump in for a conversation. This situation can arise if people need to leave early or use the restroom or take a break while the speed-meetings continue. Just make sure that when the workshop has an even number of participants, the team member removes his or her profile-sign so that others don't mistake the team member as being a potential partner to pair up with in the next round.

Avoid using a participant "lineup" during the speed-meeting process.

Team members might be tempted to form pairs for the speed-meetings by having the participants stand side-by-side in parallel lines in an effort to make finding new partners easier. Avoid this method completely. It has been tried and failed. The lineup approach prevents people from sitting down or moving around the room between speed-meeting rounds. It also is distracting because conversations are occurring in too close proximity. Some participants will prefer a quieter spot away from the larger group to engage in their speed-meeting conversations. When participants are lined up, they are in a sense prisoners of the process, unable to move away, take a break, get some water or a snack, or sit down.

LESSON LEARNED

Nonprofit representatives should be encouraged to provide as much specific information as possible to create effective profile-signs, as these will become future references for follow-up by participants and possibly other nonprofit colleagues.

LESSON LEARNED

CoLAB teams may want to be prepared to allow participants to mingle and converse after the CoLAB activities have ended and profile-signs have been collected. This may make a big difference, especially for nonprofit representatives who suffer from insufficient time for planning partnerships.

Accommodate participants who need to leave early.

Early departures are never a problem. Ensure that the participants have completed the quick feedback survey and that their profile-signs include the workshop number and their contact information. Most importantly, don't let them leave without first retrieving their profile-signs. Regardless of the situation, always sincerely thank participants for attending.

Follow up with those participants who don't complete evaluation surveys or permission forms.

Should participants forget to complete these forms, simply send them the documents, attached to an e-mail message, requesting that they complete the survey and/or permissions, the day after the workshop has taken place.

Don't despair over difficulties engaging participants postworkshop.

What happens to participants during the weeks and months following a CoLAB Workshop experience? Do they follow up with any of their fellow CoLABers? And if so, what's the story of these new meetings and relationships? Have they benefited from the resources or information they gathered during the workshop? Do CoLABers find that talking to strangers becomes easier and more routine as a result of their workshop participation? These and many other questions inevitably arise.

Unfortunately, gaining access to this hidden information isn't easy. CoLABers go on with their lives and sometimes forget that some of their new project partners were introduced to them during a CoLAB Workshop. Maybe they've moved on to other jobs, other courses, or other regions, and these life changes often can relegate the workshop experience to a distant memory. This is all to say that team members should not be disappointed if they are unsuccessful in their attempts to contact former participants as a means for learning about ways in which their attendance at a CoLAB Workshop produced beneficial results in their lives. Attribution of any such benefits may be difficult for participants to quantify or describe. Team members should consider any subsequent feedback or success stories to be unexpected gifts.

Remain calm.

In general, the goal is to deliver a workshop that creates a comfortable, stress-free environment. Participants will show up with different levels of tolerance or excitement for engaging in activities and talking with others they do not know. Instructing participants to choose partners for face-to-face interactions is in itself a very challenging activity for most people. This means that team members themselves will want to present a relaxed sense of confidence throughout the workshop. No matter what happens, the demeanor of facilitators should be consistently positive, accommodating, and receptive

---

LESSON LEARNED

Topic-based CoLABs yield the most specific evaluation data.

LESSON LEARNED

Once a CoLAB team has successfully facilitated ten two-hour CoLAB Workshops, the team may want to try adding activities that will help participants formulate more structured future plans.

to hearing the needs of participants whenever they arise. Calmly satisfying these needs or accommodating delays, lapses, or missteps will generally be preferable to allowing any level of additional stress to creep into the workshop.

The metagoal should be that once participants begin arriving, nothing that happens is labeled as "wrong," so there's no need to react negatively. Beyond the recommendations introduced in this chapter, other situations will arise that have not been anticipated by the team. Through practice, the team will learn to breathe and carry on. Remaining calm as you work through each new situation will contribute to the team's learning, producing unexpected benefits in subsequent workshops.

Envisioning the Future

Fortunately, there will never be a scarcity of strangers with whom we can interact. This means that the potential for participating in collaborative environments created during CoLAB Workshops will have many practical future applications. The more frequently these workshops are presented, the better the chances for expediting the integration of new people and ideas into our lives.

Libraries, conferences, or community foundations may become the go-to venues for convening CoLAB Workshops to help community members make valuable connections. Imagine having an idea for a project, or wanting to improve a community problem, and having the opportunity to request a CoLAB, at your library for instance, to expose hidden community resources. A simple two- or three-hour workshop or an extended twelve-hour workshop, within a few weeks of a request, may be just the perfect process to expedite the generation of innovative ideas and connections with others who care enough about the issue to show up. Consider the option of a Collaborating with Strangers Workshop presented regularly at an academic library where community residents and academics meet to learn about one another and a specific topic. Or perhaps using CoLAB activities in every classroom on the first day of school or a semester will become the norm. CoLAB Workshops could someday become commonplace in many different venues. These scenarios are not unrealistic fantasies. Rather, they offer ideal strategies for how the world can begin assimilating face-to-face collaboration workshops into communities—transforming them, one stranger at a time.

LESSON LEARNED

The core competencies for facilitators, as developed by the International Association of Facilitators (www.iaf-world .org/site/professional/ core-competencies), can provide excellent guidance for conducting successful CoLAB Workshops: "create collaborative client relationships, plan appropriate group processes, create and sustain a participatory environment, guide group to appropriate and useful outcomes, build and maintain professional knowledge, and model positive and professional attitude."

About the Authors

BESS G. DE FARBER, a nonprofit management specialist, is the grants manager for the University of Florida George A. Smathers Libraries and served in the same capacity at University of Arizona Libraries. Author of *Collaborative Grant-Seeking: A Practical Guide for Librarians*, she has provided grantsmanship instruction throughout the past twenty-eight years and has led efforts to secure millions in grant funding for nonprofits and academic libraries. Her research interest is asset-based collaboration development. As president of ASK Associates and a certified professional facilitator through the International Association of Facilitators, she created the CoLAB Planning Series, group processes serving thousands of individuals and their organizations to find new collaborative partnerships.

APRIL HINES is the journalism and mass communications librarian for the University of Florida George A. Smathers Libraries. Her research areas include inquiry-based information literacy instruction, face-to-face facilitative processes, library marketing and outreach, and social media engagement. She has presented and published on such topics as academic librarians and personal branding, using ethnic newspapers to reach underserved communities, and developing a library student ambassador program. Hines has participated on several grant projects and leads the Collaborating with Strangers In and Outside Mass Communications project sponsored by Procter & Gamble.

BARBARA J. HOOD is the director of communications for the University of Florida George A. Smathers Libraries. She promotes the libraries for academic, library, and general public communities at local, state, national, and international levels. Hood has coordinated and photographed many hundreds of library events for donors, the campus, and the local community. She has participated on several grant-awarded project teams, most notably the Institute for Museum and Library Services' National Leadership Grants project "The Panama Canal—Preserving a Legacy, Celebrating a Centennial, Leveraging an Extraordinary Human Achievement."

Index

f denotes figures; *t* denotes tables